THE NEW 42: GOD TERRAFORMS ALL THINGS

BY
ERIC ANDERSON AND
NATHAN MARCHAND

Interior Design by Nathan Marchand
Cover and Artwork by Ruth Pike-Miller

First Printing

Eric:
To my parents, Jim and Vonny Anderson, for supporting me and encouraging my faith in Christ. Thanks, Mom, for introducing me to my first fandom when I was a child!

Nathan:
To my Dad, Joseph Marchand, who spent quality time with his rambunctious son watching late-night reruns of *Star Trek*. Thanks for starting me on the path to writing and nerd-dom!

DAY 1: TERRAFORMING FROM CHRIST
BY ERIC ANDERSON

See, I am doing a new thing! Now it springs up; do you not
perceive it? I am making a way in the wilderness and streams
in the wasteland.
Isaiah 43:19

Did you really think that *42* would happen only once?
We're back, and there is a lot of terraforming to do!

"Terraforming" is a word that first appeared in 1942 in
a short story written for the magazine *Astounding Science Fiction*
entitled, "Collision Orbit." The idea is to change the entire
ecosystem of a planet to be more hospitable for a particular
species. We see this in a lot of shows and movies over the years.
Star Trek used it at the end of *Star Trek II* and showed us the
world in *Star Trek III*. The worlds visited in *Firefly* were once
terraformed. In the *Stargate SG-1* episode "Scorched Earth,"
the team travels to a planet where a ship comes along
terraforming it with fire for a sulfur-based race. Or you might
also remember that General Zod attempts to terraform Earth
in *Man of Steel*.

This is an exciting idea—a whole planet's ecosystem
being radically rebuilt—but it would also be a very big job.
Interestingly, this concept is gaining ground in theoretical
science. More and more articles are popping up about the
possibility of terraforming Mars or the moon.

Did you know that God has an interest in terraforming? Oh, Scripture does include a story about God terraforming the planet. Actually, a couple of them. We call one the Six Days of Creation, and we call another Noah's Flood. But that is not what God wants to terraform the most. We find a theme in Scripture of God stepping in and radically changing both people and cultures. This is what we'll be focusing on over the next 42 days. While we explore this, I want you to be asking yourself, "How has God terraformed me? What is He currently doing to terraform me and the community I am active within? How can I participate in this work?"

There was a line of Avengers comics called *Avengers World*. Early on in this line, Earth comes under attack from yet another group of powerful aliens. They send "terraforming bombs" to our planet from Mars. As the bombs hit, a variety of alien plants and creatures come to life and start attacking anyone they come in contact with. Of course the Avengers go fight this new enemy, but their first fight does not go well. All except Captain America are captured, and he comes back to build a whole new Avengers team with the aid of a program Tony Stark built. One of the newbs is Captain Universe, who is a personification of the universe itself. What is amazing in this story is that amid all the fighting, she stops the enemy simply by being there. The attackers, save for one, bow down to her as if she is their deity. They stop the attack because she says so. Their hearts are changed not by battle or banter, but by experiencing whom they thought was a deity.

In real life, the universe has no personification. It is simply a thing, albeit a very large thing. But the Creator of this universe—including our amazing planet with DNA coding and a great oxygen cycle, as well as gravity, the stars, and the other galaxies—this same creator wants to meet with you and terraform your heart. You see, humanity is full of sin. We ignore the commands of our creator and choose terrible acts and thoughts. Our sin puts a horrid atmosphere in the way. Having paid your debt on the cross, Jesus wants to communicate with you and reveal Himself to you through the Bible and the Holy Spirit. Sometimes He will even use circumstances. In so doing He will change you from a sinner into a loving, self-controlled, and gentle human.

In the previous *42*, we introduced you to Him. In this book we want you to learn the history of His work in the world. Along the way we'll have some fun with aliens, warriors, ninjas, robots, and other characters.

Quest of the Day

1. Read Romans 12.
2. Ask God to prepare your heart for the next 42 days.
3. If you do not already have a journal, please get one for this study. There will sometimes be questions for you

to ponder and journaling is a good way to do so. You might also consider sharing your thoughts with friends along the way.

4. Journal about your expectations for this study.

DAY 2: CRISIS ON FLASHPOINT REBIRTHS
BY NATHAN MARCHAND

There is a time for everything,
and a season for every activity under heaven....
Ecclesiastes 3:1

"Worlds will live. Worlds will die. And the DC Universe will never be the same!"

So proclaimed the tagline for *Crisis on Infinite Earths*, a 12-part "maxi-series" written by Marv Wolfman and illustrated by George Pérez. Published monthly from 1985-1986, it became the first of the (in)famous reboots DC Comics would do every few decades (give or take five years).

It certainly lived up to the hype. All but one Earth in the multiverse was consumed by the Anti-Monitor, an evil, nigh-omnipotent being from beyond time and space. Barry Allan (the second Flash) and Supergirl, along with many other characters, died. Afterward, all of DC's comics were relaunched with a new streamlined continuity. Superman became the sole survivor of Krypton's destruction. Wally West inherited his uncle's mantle as the Flash. Wonder Woman was relaunched from the ground up. And that's just what it did to *those* characters. It was, however, embraced by fans, who loved *Crisis* and the new stories.

The same couldn't be said for 2011's *Flashpoint*, DC's second reboot. The series written by Geoff Johns and illustrated by Andy Kubert radically altered the DC Universe and spun into the New 52 (where do you think we got the title of this devotional?), a rebranding of DC's comics. All 52 of their titles (hence the name) were relaunched with new number one issues, starting with the *Justice League*. Unfortunately, readers and fans were vexed by the radical, often inconsistent changes made to their favorite characters.

This led to a softer relaunch in 2016 with *DC Universe: Rebirth*, a one-shot comic written by Geoff Johns. This made DC's characters more like their pre-New 52 versions. Fans were delighted, to say the least.

Reboots have become a fact of life. We see them not only on the comic stands but also on TV and in the cinema. They remind us that the one constant in the universe is change. Sometimes these changes are for the better (marriage, birth of a child) and sometimes they're for the worse (a death in the family, job loss). It's in those hard changes that we get nostalgic for the "good old days" and long for how things used to be. Or we strive to make positive changes hoping our lives will stay the same after we achieve them.

King Solomon, the likely author of Ecclesiastes, reminds us that while change, both good and bad, is unavoidable, it is appointed by God.

There is a time for everything,

and a season for every activity under heaven...

(Ecclesiastes 3:1)

Life works in cycles. Nothing is permanent. That's both terrifying and comforting. You may mourn the loss of a friend or family member today, but tomorrow you may celebrate the birth of a child. There may be peace today, but war could break out tomorrow. You can quit one job and move on to a better one. You could be plucked out of one timeline and dropped into a new one where your mother never died (okay, maybe not that one). Ups and downs. Highs and lows. I should know. I've lost jobs, gigs, family members, friends, and girlfriends. However, I also sought all of those in the first place because I needed new things in my life.

Through it all, remember that Jesus Christ is walking with you. Nothing comes into your life unless He allows it. He will not abandon you as you navigate these changes. He'll give you the strength to shoulder the bad ones and the wisdom to handle the good ones, no matter how drastic they are.

Perhaps you're reading this book because you want a change in your life or the life of someone you know. Maybe you've been praying for a spouse, a job, or someone's salvation. I can't promise those specific requests will happen, but I can assure you change is coming. It always is. But through Christ, good can come from every change.

7

Even when your favorite superhero is turned into a jerk after an insane "event comic."

Quest of the Day

1. Read Ecclesiastes 3.

2. Write down an example from your own life of each of the "a time for…" verses. (Example: "A time to weep" could be when a relative died and "a time to laugh" could be a funny childhood memory).

3. What changes do you want to see in your life? Write them down and pray about them. I encourage you to share these and other insights you gain from this 42-day study on social media with the hashtag #42Terraform.

DAY 3: SIX DAYS OF TERRAFORMING
BY ERIC ANDERSON

In the beginning God created....
Genesis 1:1a

Customization is a significant part of gaming. Maybe you are a huge *Minecraft* fan. It is amazing how these little digital blocks have taken over our culture. You can make whatever you want: spaceships, castles, forests, and whole towns. The craziest Minecraft creation I have seen is a recreation of Noah's Ark. Several people collaborated and spent months working on it. It was huge! Even in other games like shooters, we can customize characters with different weapons, armor, and paint jobs, etc. When the Nintendo Wii came out, creating your avatar—a "Mii"—was a big deal since you could give them any of many different hair or face options.

Tabletop gaming has had this kind of sandbox customization for much longer. Just ask any fan of Warhammer 40K or other buildable miniatures games that allow you to build your own terrain and mix and match parts of units. Historical miniature games have a long history of recreating battles with precision-built terrain and hand-painted miniatures. I enjoy creating boards for a collectible miniatures game called Heroscape. This game uses tiles that interconnect and stack on top of each other. There are also some trees, bridges and other terrain pieces you can get to build your world. I once built a board with two towers on either side of water with a bridge interconnecting them. It was a cool map and my cousin and I had a great time battling on it.

Perhaps you create video games or board games or card games. Some indie designers produce it all, including sound, graphics, and story. Do you design levels, write music, or craft stories for them? *Minecraft* is a great example of forming something with many layers and changing what you built to better suit your purposes.

Creating is a significant aspect of human life. We build houses, schools, roads, fire trucks, hospitals, and many other necessities. But we also like to play around, don't we? That is why Legos and painting canvases are important. As a lighting designer, I work with several dimensions such as position, color, pattern, movement, and so on to create scenes for various events.

Genesis 1 starts out by telling us that, "In the beginning, God created the heavens and the earth." Yet, He wasn't done. His Spirit covered the formless planet. He did specific projects each day. We call these the Six Days of Creation. He had created the Earth, but much of Creation still needed terraforming. Some things were new, but He changed the biosphere by adding various layers. He started with light and then formed the sky (or our atmosphere). He cleared water away to make land and covered it with vegetation. Eventually, God made stars, the moon, fish, birds, mammals, reptiles, and even these odd creatures called humans. For whatever reason God chose not to tell us what He did on other planets. He simply wants us to understand His story of working with us. If aliens exist, maybe someday He will tell us about His story with them or how they interact with this story.

What do we learn about humans? First, we learn that we are *very good* in God's eyes. Don't let others insult you. You are part of the only creation Genesis stresses as being *very good*. The other parts, such as water and light and animals, were good; just not very good. Take honor in being called "*very good*" by your creator. Second, we He made us in His image. This is key. This is why we like creating new stories and inventions and games and so many other things! We get that from Him. We also get our desire for extending grace and finding truth from Him.

Genesis 2 gives us a different view. It gives us a close-up view of His work creating us. What does this mean? Well, the writer is stressing that creating us was personal. God didn't give the work to robots and machines. He was personally involved in crafting our species in a hands on approach. Not only that, but He took a portion of the planet and planted a special Garden there. As a creative, I wonder what flowers and even animals He put in the Garden of Eden that we no longer see. Can you imagine how pristine this was? Imagine yourself as Adam or Eve exploring this place for the first time, naming plants, creatures, and finding strange little insects.

God personally crafted your skills, height, hair, etc. When you play with Legos, create new structures in *Minecraft*, or explore new digital worlds, think about how God crafted your world. Imagine why He might have designed DNA as He did or the way He created light to interact with objects and shadows. Remember, you are active in a grand story!

Quest of the Day

1. Read Genesis chapters 1 and 2.
2. Use Legos or unexpected media or materials to create a piece as worship to God. You could even do something in *Minecraft* for this. Post a picture of it with the hashtag #42Terraforming.

DAY 4: FORBIDDEN ALCHEMY
BY NATHAN MARCHAND

And the Lord God commanded the man, "You are free to eat
from any tree in the garden; but you must not eat from the
tree of the knowledge of good and evil, for when you eat
from it you will certainly die."
Genesis 2:16-17

In the anime/manga *Full Metal Alchemist*, Edward and
Alphonse Elric are precocious children with exceptional
talents in alchemy, "the scientific technique of understanding
the structure of matter, decomposing it, and then
reconstructing it." Sadly, their father departs suddenly, leaving
the Elric brothers alone with their mother. The boys love their
mother, who is delighted by their prowess with alchemy, so
they are happy despite their father essentially abandoning
them.

But, as often happens in comic books, tragedy strikes.
Mrs. Elric becomes ill and dies. Grief-stricken, the boys
dedicate themselves to studying human transmutation, the
greatest taboo in alchemy, to resurrect their mother. The
foundational law of alchemy is Equivalent Exchange, which
states, "In order to obtain or create something, something of
equal value must be lost or destroyed." However, to
paraphrase Jesus, "What can anyone give in exchange for [a]
soul?" (Matt. 16:26; Mark 8:37).

Despite this, Ed and Al attempt a human transmutation—with ugly results. The boys are pulled into the Gate, where they meet a terrifying being called Truth. He tells them they had dared to cross into God's domain. Ed loses his left leg in exchange for absorbing vast amounts of knowledge on alchemy. When he returns to Earth, he sees what is supposed to be his mother—an abomination that doesn't live long. Worse yet, Al is taken, body and soul, in exchange. Ed, unwilling to lose his brother, performs another transmutation, sacrificing his arm to recover his brother's soul and graft it to a suit of armor.

For the rest of the series, their goal is to restore the bodies they lost and prevent other such abuses of alchemy.

In the Garden of Eden, God gave Adam and Eve only one law: do not eat from the Tree of the Knowledge of Good and Evil "or you will surely die." It was an easy law to obey; Eden was full of many trees with delightful fruit. But Genesis 3:1 tells us Satan, the "ancient serpent" (Rev. 12:9), appealed to Eve with his silver tongue, saying, "Did God really say, 'You must not eat from any tree in the garden'?" He promised that if she and her husband ate of the fruit they would be like God, knowing good and evil.

These words led humanity to commit its first sin. They did indeed garner knowledge—and shame. Adam and Eve used fig leaves to hide their nakedness—and their sin—from

God. But He saw through it. God banished them from Eden to keep them from eating from the tree of life and becoming immortal, setting an angel with a flaming sword to guard it.

In exchange for the forbidden fruit, Adam and Eve gave their innocence. They paid the price for violating God's only taboo, and now all their descendants—you, me, Eric, and every human who's ever lived—have been born with a sin nature. As the Apostle Paul said in Romans 5:12, "...sin entered the world through one man, and death through sin, and in this way death came to all people, because all sinned." Like the Elric Brothers, we live with the consequences of sin while searching for a means of redemption.

Thankfully, that redemption came in the form of Jesus Christ (but that's a story for a later entry).

Quest of the Day

1. Read Genesis 3 and Romans 5.
2. As difficult as it may be to admit to yourself, write down the sins you struggle with the most. Get to the heart of the matter by discovering why you commit these sins. You may try to tell yourself your motives are good (like Ed and Al did), but these are nothing but excuses ("fig leaves," so to speak).
3. Confess these sins before God in prayer. Remember He is more than willing to forgive a penitent heart.

Day 5: Cain and Hawkgirl are Traitors!
By Eric Anderson

"What have you done? Listen! Your brother's blood cries out
to me from the ground."
Genesis 4:10

Is betrayal the most depraved act? Or is murder? Both of these things started together. After the Fall into sin, Eve gave birth to a couple of sons named Cain and Abel. Both gave offerings to God. Cain was a farmer, so he brought fruit or grain. Abel, who worked with various animals, brought a sacrifice of fat portions. God was happy with the fat, not so happy with the fruit. Later, Cain acted in jealousy by taking Abel for a walk. Only one of them came back. This was the first murder and the first human betrayal. Do you think Abel saw it coming?

The Justice League doesn't see it coming. In a three-episode story arc at the end of the cartoon's second season, we find Thanagar invading Earth. Thanagar is the homeworld of Hawkgirl and seems friendly enough. They came here to protect us from their evil enemies, who had just scouted Earth, but they have an endgame they aren't sharing. Hawkgirl has been spying on Earth and transmitting her findings to her homeworld. They know exactly how to take down the other six members of the League. She betrays her best friends and even Green Lantern John Stewart, her boyfriend. They had no clue she was spying or that she is betrothed to someone in the army of Thanagar. She told them she was lost with no way to get home. But she was gathering info the whole time so Thanagar could invade and take the Earth. Using her information, the invaders capture the entire League, take away John's ring and gear from some of the others, and take domain over the planet.

Can you imagine being in John Stewart's place? Your girlfriend told someone how to take you down. She handed your planet over to this huge army, led by the guy she is engaged to marry? Now, think about Abel. How did he feel when Cain attacked him? No one had killed another person before. How did this happen?

Betrayal rips a person to the core, yet even here God was at work to give mercy to Cain. He confronted him, cursing him in the process. He took away Cain's skill for working with plants and agriculture. Cain pleaded with God. "No, this is too much for me!" So God, in His mercy, put a mark on Cain for protection so that no one could take vengeance on him. God was expecting man to forgive even something as bad as murder. What I find extraordinary is that even after this, God let Cain have a good life. He married, had kids, and even built a city. He still participated in leadership and helped shape life and culture on Earth.

What happens to Hawkgirl? First, she brings John his ring back and helps the team fight off the invaders. She chooses to leave the League after helping them fight off the army she served. *Justice League Unlimited* eventually let us know that she goes to Dr. Fate's lair, where she has more adventures, and after that is reinstated into the League. But it is a hard road of reconciliation. Some people are still angry with her.

We do not know the process that Adam and Eve went through as their sons fought. We don't know how God worked in their lives, but we do know that Jesus cares about both forgiveness and reconciliation. If you betrayed someone, don't be afraid to seek reconciliation. If you have been betrayed, remember that Jesus urged us to forgive others in many of his teachings. Either way, seek reconciliation, for as Jesus said in Luke 6:27-28, "Love your enemies, do good to those who hate you, bless those who curse you, pray for those who mistreat you."

Quest of the Day

1. Read Genesis 4:1-18.
2. Read John 21:15-25 where Jesus reinstates Peter after disowning Him.
3. Journal your thoughts about reconciliation.

DAY 6: THE BANISHED THUNDER GOD
BY NATHAN MARCHAND

"I am going to bring floodwaters on the earth to destroy all life under the heavens, every creature that has the breath of life in it. Everything on earth will perish. But I will establish my covenant with you, and you will enter the ark—you and your sons and your wife and your sons' wives with you."
Genesis 6:17-18

Like most of the characters in the Marvel Cinematic Universe, Thor's 2011 film catapulted him from semi-obscure superhero to rock star. In it, Thor, Prince of Asgard, journeys to Jotunheim to retrieve the Casket of Ancient Winters, which had been stolen by the Frost Giants. The ensuing battle endangers the fragile truce between Asgard and Jotunheim, so Thor's father, Odin, strips him of his power and banishes him to Earth as a mortal. By the end of the film, Thor learns a hard lesson about humility.

The comics that inspired this film go even deeper, though. In the film, Thor was mortal, but he was a strong, super-buff mortal. In *Thor* #159, we learn Thor became the frail medical student Donald Blake with no memory of his godhood. The hands that once slew the Birdbeast and fought Storm Giants now healed the sick as a surgeon.

But, as seen in Thor's first appearance in *Journey Into Mystery* #83, Stan Lee writes a story both ironic and genius.

Donald Blake, on a visit to Norway, retreats into a cave to elude the titular "Stone Men of Saturn." There, having lost his cane, he finds a walking stick that he tries to use to roll away a stone. Lightning flashes, and the stick transforms—as does he. Donald Blake becomes the mighty Thor, and the stick is now Mjolnir, a hammer inscribed with this now famous enchantment:

Whosoever holds this hammer,

If he be worthy,

Shall possess the power of Thor.

Thor uses the powers granted him by Mjolnir to defeat the Stone Men. However, he's plagued by doubts as to whether he is Donald Blake or the God of Thunder. That is until the fateful issue when Odin reveals everything. Thor learns humility and his identity is restored.

In Genesis 6, it's recorded that God was grieved by humanity's wickedness (Genesis 6:6). He says, "I will wipe from the face of the earth the human race I have created—and with them the animals, the birds and the creatures that move along the ground—for I regret that I have made them" (v. 7). You can feel the anguish in those words. God, who is altogether holy and can't abide sin, felt like He must wipe the slate clean.

Then we read, "But Noah found favor in the eyes of the Lord" (v. 8).

Noah and his family remained righteous amidst the rampant evil. Because of this, God instructed them to build an ark to house themselves and two of every kind of animal to survive the flood He would use to punish humanity. They obeyed, and a few chapters later, they emerged from the huge boat on dry land. Now they had a renewed world to explore and cultivate.

Just as Odin disguised Mjolnir as a walking stick for Thor amidst his banishment, so God provided Noah with an ark to escape the coming judgment. When they exited the ark, God put a rainbow in the sky (kinda like the Bifrost, you could say), which symbolized His promise never to destroy the world with a flood again.

Perhaps you feel like God's hand of judgment is heavy upon you. However, God is also gracious. Even amidst His discipline, He will bless you with refined character and new strength. There's always purpose in hardship for those who are in Christ.

Who knows—you may find Thor's hammer hidden in the hardship.

Quest of the Day

1. Read Genesis 6-9.

2. Is God disciplining you? Are you struggling with the consequences of your sins? Journal about this, writing out what you did and what has come from it.

3. After this, journal about how God has been gracious to you during this disciplinary time. This is good to do to avoid growing bitter toward Him.

DAY 7: PRAYER DAY

This is one of four prayer days throughout this study. The focus on these days is not to do a lot of reading, but to help you carve out a space to communicate with Christ on your own. We will give you some prompts based on the few days leading up to these days and encourage you to ask God for further depth of what is being spoken into you in this study.

Take a few minutes for silence. Sit, listen to God, give Him an opportunity to speak with you. Be ready to write some things down so you can look back at it later. This helps with the question, "Did God really say that?"

In the recent days you learned about our sin, God's discipline, and His mercy. You are invited now to communicate with God about this further.

Spend some time worshiping Christ. Thank God for some of the nature around us or for His blessings in your life, whatever they are.

Ask God if there is anything you need to confess. Take some time in silence it listen for his answer. Confession sounds like a big word but is just a way of agreeing with God that sin is sin. Take some time for confession. It might sound similar to this:

God I have sinned through actions, words and thoughts. Sometimes I have sinned by inaction when you wanted me to do something. Please forgive me. I want to be a better example of you to those around me. Thank you for mercy and please give me strength to do better.

Have you betrayed anyone? Has someone betrayed you? Talk with God about the situation. Pray about seeking reconciliation. Let God brainstorm with you for this effort.

On day six, you had the chance to journal about God's discipline and mercy in your life. Take some time for discussion with God about this. Ask Him to show you pictures of what it looks like to live without sin.

Spend a few more moments in prayer. God may have more to say to you. Remember to pray for family and friends, especially if they are going through difficult situations.

DAY 8: THE UNIVERSAL MIND
BY NATHAN MARCHAND

Then they said, "Come, let us build ourselves a city, with a tower that reaches to the heavens, so that we may make a name for ourselves and not be scattered over the face of the whole earth."
Genesis 11:4

Skagra didn't want to conquer the universe. No, he would *be* the universe.

In the infamously incomplete (but now restored) 1979 *Doctor Who* episode "Shada" written by Douglas Adams (so you know a book titled *42* has to cover it), the aforementioned villain plans to drain the minds of all sentient beings in the universe and replace them with his own. The Universal Mind. Obviously, he doesn't think small.

Brilliant though Skagra is, he seeks the legendary Time Lord criminal Salyavin, who could implant his mind into others, an ability Skagra wants to combine with his brain-draining sphere. Salyavin is being held on the prison planet Shada. Unfortunately, its location only is recorded in the book *The Worshipful and Ancient Law of Gallifrey*, a lost artifact that now belongs to Chronotis, a retired absent-minded Time Lord living as a Cambridge professor. Luckily for Chronotis, he's visited by the Doctor (played by the great

Tom Baker) and his Time Lady Companion, Romana. What follows is a series of shenanigans involving the professor misplacing the powerful book by giving it to a student, an invisible starship (because budget cuts), Skagra brain-draining the Doctor, and the revelation that Chronotis is Salyavin.

Eventually, all parties converge on the titular prison planet. Skagra unleashes lumbering monsters called Krargs and several mind-controlled prisoners to fight the heroes while he searches for Salyavin. The truth about the Galifreyan criminal is soon revealed, and the Doctor reminds his foe that his (the Doctor's) mind is also trapped in the spheres. Skagra retreats to his ship, where he's taken prisoner by his own computer because the Doctor convinced it to side with him. Skagra is left to hear stories of the Doctor for eternity.

While Skagra's plot is the sort of preposterous plan that could only be concocted on Classic *Doctor Who*, his ambition is nothing new. In Genesis 11:1-9, humanity settled in Shinar and undertook the construction of a glorious city with a tower called a ziggurat. "Come, let us build ourselves a city, with a tower that reaches to the heavens, so that we may make a name for ourselves and not be scattered over the face of the whole earth" (Genesis 11:4). They shared a common language and culture, so there were no barriers preventing them from undertaking this project.

Now, you may think, "Isn't it good to be united under a common goal?" Yes, but in this case humanity was attempting to take control of its own destiny. They were made in God's image, yet in their pride they sought equality with God. The Triune God knew the incredible capabilities and potential of humanity and sought to hinder them: "If as one people speaking the same language they have begun to do this, then nothing they plan to do will be impossible for them. Come, let us go down and confuse their language so they will not understand each other" (Genesis 11:6-7). So, for the first time, humanity didn't speak the same language, and the building stopped. Those who understood one another gathered together and spread across the world.

Skagra was a brilliant man who believed he should encompass the universe. He sought the power to make it so. The universe was a few thousand years away from coming under Skagra's hive-mind control. It wasn't until the Doctor used the copy of his mind in Skagra's spheres to confuse his minions and then manipulate the villain's computer that his ambitions were brought to a halt.

The thing is, we've all at one point tried to be Skagra or build our own Tower of Babel. The sin of pride is literally believing you can do anything and don't need God. Scripture warns us time and again that "[p]ride goes before destruction, a haughty spirit before a fall" (Proverbs 16:18). You may be talented and powerful, but you are nothing without God. He gave you those abilities, and He can take them away. If you set out on your own, no matter how noble your goals may be, if you pursue them without God, He will oppose them. But it is for your own good. Sometimes it takes having our ambitions frustrated to bring us into submission to God. Jesus said in Matthew 23:12 and Luke 14:11, "For whoever exalts himself will be humbled, and whoever humbles himself will be exalted."

Don't be like Skagra, or you may suddenly find yourself speaking gibberish!

Quest of the Day

1. Read Genesis 11:1-9.
2. What are your biggest goals? Write them down. If you have pursued any past goals apart from God, repent of these selfish ambitions.
3. Pray for all of these and ask God if He wants to add any to your list. Regardless, dedicate them to Him.

DAY 9: ABRAHAM AND THE BULLETPROOF MONK
BY ERIC ANDERSON

"…your name will be Abraham for I have made you a father
of many nations."
Genesis 17:5

He is called the Monk with No Name. He left his home years ago to study at a monastery. He did not lose his name— he gave it up willingly. As the "Bulletproof Monk," he now protects an ancient scroll of knowledge. He fulfilled three prophecies that included fighting for love under a palace of jade, fighting for justice while a flock of cranes circle above, and rescuing friends he has never met with a family he never knew he had. He doesn't give up his name for nothing or a wish to be called something else; he relinquishes it for a new purpose. The temple that he trains in is destroyed by Nazis and he spends his life traveling to evade them. *Bulletproof Monk*, the movie, is based on a comic of the same name written by Brett Lewis, R.A. Jones, and Gothom Chopra with art by Michael Avon Oeming. The adaptation starred Chow Yun Fat, Sean Willian Scott, and Jamie King.

Changing names is common in Scripture, as we will see in this study. Names held a more significant role in the ancient world than today. Sometimes it was an expression of the hopes or even the feelings of the parents. They were considered a massive influence on who a person was and what they could accomplish.

Abram was one such man who had his name changed for a purpose. The story is found in Genesis 17. Abram is well along in years. God appeared to him and said "...this is my covenant with you: you will be the father of many nations. No longer will you be called Abram; your name will be Abraham, for I have made you a father of many nations" (17:4-5). Before this, God called Abram to leave his home without telling him where to go. Later, he fought to rescue his nephew, Lot, when a raiding party took him and many of his (Lot's) party. Abram was not perfect. He lied about his wife, claiming she was his sister, just because he was afraid being killed by the Pharaoh over her.

Abram means "exalted father." This in itself is high praise, don't you think? That is its own calling to live up to. Yet Abraham means "father of many." It represents that he is not just a good father, but that he would be a father of many nations and ethnic groups.

What does it mean to be a father of many nations? We know that Abraham's two sons became the peoples we know today as the Arabs and the Jews, but I don't think that was it. Years later, Abraham was given another test: sacrificing his son, Isaac. God did stop the sacrifice at the last second and then relayed this promise: "...through your offspring all nations on Earth shall be blessed, because you have obeyed me" (Gen. 22:18). The intent of the sacrifice order had never been to kill Isaac. God loved him and all humanity. It was to see if Abraham trusted God with his family and the dream of becoming a great people.

God has callings and purposes for all of us. Maybe for you it is working with kids or feeding the hungry. Perhaps he will call you to leave your home for a new land to share the Gospel to a new people group. But did you notice something about Abraham's experience? He was regularly visited by God throughout his life and built a relationship with Him. At the end of the *Bulletproof Monk* movie, it is not one person who becomes the next monk, but a romantic pair. They have a unique relationship that gives them a particular advantage. Even finding the next monk involved training and building a relationship. Much like this "Bulletproof Monk couple," God's adventures for Abraham came out of the relationship, but they also fed the relationship.

Newness comes with purpose. You find a new purpose and everything changes. We do have a series of ancient, powerful scrolls to teach us. We call this Scripture and they are collected in the Holy Bible. God's ultimate purpose for us is relationship with Him, but within that there will be other purposes. People only you can reach. Missions for you to accomplish. Have you spent enough time with Him to discern something of your mission?

<u>Quest of the Day</u>

1. Read Genesis 17-18 and 22:1-19.

2. How was Abraham's relationship with God intertwined with his mission for God?

3. Spend time in prayer with God developing your main mission (relationship with Him) and asking about sub-missions He might have for you.

DAY 10: ELEVEN REJECTED FOR ELEVEN BROTHERS
BY NATHAN MARCHAND

"You intended to harm me, but God intended it for good to
accomplish what is now being done, the saving of many
lives."
Genesis 50:20

She was just a little girl. A little girl with extraordinary
abilities named Jane. But to everyone besides her mother, she
was only Eleven.

The breakout character from *Stranger Things* is the
daughter of a woman who volunteered for a secret government
experiment trying to create mind control techniques. She is
born with psychokinetic powers. Shortly after her birth, she is
kidnapped by Dr. Martin Brenner and taken to a lab in
Hawkins, Indiana. (A show about interdimensional
Lovecraftian horrors set in my home state—I'm both excited
and terrified). Appointing himself her "father," Dr. Brenner
spends years subjecting Eleven to torturous experiments. She
is made to crush soda cans or manipulate animals. The strain
gives her nosebleeds, which only please her surrogate father.
Whenever she fails, she is locked in a solitary cell for hours.

Eventually, Eleven opens a gateway to another
dimension, unleashing a terrifying monster later dubbed the
Demogorgon. She escapes during the chaos, meeting a group
of middle school gamers led by a boy named Mike. While

Mike's friends distrust her, he has compassion on her, teaching her to speak and hiding her from authorities. He even helps her discover her taste for Eggo waffles. She'd never known such companionship. When Mike's friends reject her out of fear, he sticks by her.

The group truly rallies around her when she uses her powers to contact their missing friend, Will, who'd vanished into the otherworldly dimension they called "the Upside Down." They embark on a quest to find him, taking a reluctant Eleven with them. They take shelter in Hawkins Middle School, where they confront the Demogorgon. Eleven disintegrates the monster and vanishes into the Upside Down. She is believed dead (until season two, anyway).

In the Bible, there's a remarkable youth whose story is so much like Eleven's it's uncanny: Joseph. He was Jacob's favorite son. Like Eleven, God gifted him with special powers; in his case, prophetic dreams and the ability to interpret them. In Genesis 37, he told his brothers about his dreams where their wheat sheaves bowed to his and another where the sun, moon, and stars bowed to him. This meant he would one day rule them despite being the youngest. So, his jealous brothers secretly sold him as a slave and told their father he had been killed by a wild animal. He was rejected by his own family like Eleven was.

Joseph was taken to Egypt. Through a series of inexplicable events involving resisting the wiles of his master's wife, being sent to prison, and interpreting the dreams of the Pharaoh's baker and cupbearer, he found himself in the presence of the Egyptian ruler (Genesis 41). Pharaoh had been suffering from disturbing dreams his wise men couldn't understand, but Joseph explained that the dreams prophesied seven years of plenty followed by seven years of famine. Pharaoh was so impressed, he gave Joseph his signet ring and appointed him the second most powerful man in the land.

Joseph managed the storage of crops during the years of plenty. When famine struck, Joseph's brothers journeyed to Egypt to find food. They met Joseph but didn't recognize him. After some dealings, Joseph revealed himself to them. His entire clan settled in Egypt. Joseph's story ends with him reassuring his brothers he wouldn't seek vengeance on them: "You intended to harm me, but God intended it for good to accomplish what is now being done, the saving of many lives" (Genesis 50:20).

Perhaps you've been used, abused, and rejected by people who should care about you. The loneliness and pain are excruciating. God designed us to be communal beings, so we desire fellowship and acceptance. To be cast out from a group can feel like death. But as Eleven and Joseph show us, there is newness after rejection. God can bring you into a new tribe, a new family. Psalm 68:6a tells us, "God sets the lonely in families." Your rejection is part of God's plan. He needs to take you to where he needs you. If Eleven hadn't met Mike and the boys, she wouldn't have been able to defeat the Demogorgon. Joseph had to be sold as a slave so he would be in the right place at the right time to save millions from the famine. It doesn't make the time in between any easier, but you can go forward knowing God will see you through it and trust in His plan.

God has an incredible way of turning things around for the good of those who love Him (Romans 8:28) even if their lives are turned *upside down*.

<u>Quest of the Day</u>

1. Read Genesis 37, 39-41, 50.

2. Journal about a time you were rejected. Are you still angry? Take that anger to God in prayer and release it to him. After you do that, take a step back and ask God to show you how it fits into His larger plan for your life.

3. Write a list of lessons you learned from this rejection and how you have or can use them to help others. It's through hardship that we gain wisdom.

DAY 11: A NEW HOME
BY ERIC ANDERSON

A father to the fatherless, a defender of widows, is God in his
holy dwelling.
Psalm 68:5

Imagine growing up in the Egyptian palace. You are an adopted son of the princess and part of Pharaoh's court, but you are not Egyptian. You experience royal life and get some military training. Or maybe not. Maybe the Pharaoh does not trust you. Then it all changes. You kill someone—an Egyptian—because he was mistreating one of one of the people from whom you had been taken, who are all slaves. What would you do? Where would you go? Such is the story of Moses. He ran.

In the show *Stargate Atlantis*, Ronin Dex is also a runner. He's a military man from the planet Sateda, but his planet is overrun by an evil race called the Wraith, who love to consume the life energy of humans. They turn him into a runner, which means they hunted him for sport. He has a tracker on him, so any place he went, they went, and the fight would overwhelm that area. Eventually, a team from Atlantis comes through the Stargate, an ancient device used to travel between planets, and finds him. He kidnaps Teyla and Commander Shephard so they can take the tracker out of him.

After it is resolved, they offer him a home, and he becomes part of the team. For the first time he didn't have to run from anything or to anything (of course he still ran into fights).

Both Ronin and Moses were men of action. Moses went into the wilderness, specifically to a land called Midian. Here, he found some sisters who were bringing their flock to drink from a well. When some shepherds from a different group started pushing the women and their flocks around, he went into action, fought them off, and watered the flocks for the girls. After this, their father invited him to join the family and gave him a wife. He finally had a family, but was he really home?

We all struggle with finding a home. Some of us lack a mom or a dad or both. Some have plenty of family but few friends, or at least not a core group of friends to count on. In a world of mobile devices, when we should be closer, we end up being further apart. Fulfillment seems hard to find in our overly electronic culture. We are so focused on screens that we don't get to know each other. This is one of the reasons for the growth in board games. It brings people together face to face for community and connection.

Now, after Moses had been with this new family for many years (it is traditionally accepted that it was 40 years) he found a strange sight: a burning bush that was not burning up. It was on fire, but it wasn't being eaten by the fire. As he went closer God called to him from the burning bush with a new mission: to bring His people out of slavery.

"Do not come any closer." God said. "Take off your sandals, for the place you are standing is holy ground" (Ex. 3:5). Earlier we are told that "the angel of the Lord appeared to him in the flames of fire in a bush." Any time the word "the" is in front of "angel of the Lord" we are getting a glimpse of Jesus at work in the Old Testament. The new home is the presence of God. The one consistent home and help available is the presence of God Himself. Moses regularly had meetings alone with God. He did it for 40 days before he came down the mountain with the Ten Commandments. Throughout his time leading the Israelites in the desert, he would often go into the Tent of Meeting to talk to God and come out with a face so vibrant that his people required him to wear a veil. For another 40 years he led the Israelites through the wilderness. As they travelled he consistently met with God for wisdom, instruction, and guidance. God is omnipresent, which means he is everywhere and always available. He is better than a yacht, a motorhome, or even a Stargate. He is in every ocean trench, high mountain, and distant planet. We just have to look for Him.

Quest of the Day

1. Read Exodus 1:11-25.

2. How has God become a home for you? Post a thought about this online with the hashtag #42Terraforming.

3. Do you ever ask God to be with you? Take some quiet time to converse with God about this concept of Him being your home.

DAY 12: A TALE OF TWO SHEPHERDS
BY NATHAN MARCHAND

"And now the cry of the Israelites has reached me, and I have
seen the way the Egyptians are oppressing them. So now, go.
I am sending you to Pharaoh to bring my people the Israelites
out of Egypt."
Exodus 3:9-10

"A part of Shepherd Book is artificial," wrote Chris
Ullrich for *ComicMix*. "He found God in a bowl of soup. Book
is best known for his greatest failure."

Shepherd Derrial Book is the beloved spiritual teacher
aboard the starship Serenity on the TV series *Firefly*. A devout
Christian, he is seemingly the odd man out on a ship whose
crew consists of smugglers, con artists, fugitives, and a glorified
prostitute. What the Serenity crew doesn't know is Book's old
life, before that fateful day with a bowl of chicken soup, was
marked by violence.

In the comic book spin-off, *Serenity: The Shepherd's Tale*,
Book is born Henry Evans. After growing up with an abusive
father, he becomes a thief and catches the attention of the
Independence Movement (aka the Browncoats), a confederacy
of planets seeking to break away from the ruling Alliance. After
honing his combat skills for years, the directionless Evans
volunteers to take part in a long-term mole operation against
the Alliance. This required a new identity, so Evans lures a

41

young man named Derrial Book into an alleyway and murders him, the thief assuming the youth's name and identity.

After rising through the Alliance ranks in only a few years, he becomes an officer aboard the I.A.V. Cortez and directs risky raids on multiple Independence facilities on six planets—only for his Alliance forces to be ambushed. Thousands of lives are lost. It is known as "single greatest disaster in Alliance history." Book is discharged. Without his position in the Alliance military, he is forgotten by the Browncoats.

He spends years as a vagabond. Beaten by an Alliance police officer, Book wakes up in what is presumably a homeless shelter. He's offered a bowl of chicken soup. Book stares into it, pondering life, the universe, and everything. "The universe. Existence. All of creation supports this bowl. Which supports the soup. Which supports me. It gives me life." With renewed purpose, he exits the shelter and joins the Southdown Abbey. Ten years later, he leaves the abbey to become a missionary. That same day, he meets Serenity's captain, Malcolm Reynolds.

Book's story parallels that of one of the Old Testament's greatest heroes: Moses. In the first few chapters of Exodus, we learn that Israel had been enslaved by Egypt after the death of Joseph. Fearing that the Hebrew population was too large, Pharaoh decreed that every Hebrew boy must be thrown into the Nile after birth. When Moses was born, his mother saw he was no ordinary child and, ironically, set him in a basket and let him float down the Nile. More ironically, he was found by Pharaoh's daughter and raised in the Egyptian palace. So, like Shepherd Book, he came to an unexpected position of power.

Years later, Moses killed an Egyptian beating one of fellow Hebrews. He was scorned by his people for this, and once word reached Pharaoh, Moses fled into a self-imposed exile to avoid the ruler's wrath. He spent the next forty years in Midian working as a shepherd (though a different one from Book).

Moses probably would've been content with this life, but just as Book had an epiphany with a bowl of soup, Moses had a turning point with something even more extraordinary: a burning bush. This bush was a manifestation of God Himself. He told Moses He had chosen him to free the Hebrews from Egypt. Moses was reluctant (like the hero of any classic story), but after some dramatic signs involving a leprous hand and a snake, Moses accepted his new mission.

Have you ever had a "bowl of soup" or "burning bush" moment? Sometimes these are dramatic events, like with Moses, but most of the time they're quiet and seemingly ordinary like with Book. God works however He chooses and in the way He knows will get His people to act. Regardless, this might've come after a time of hardship and failure. You might've been lost or settled for an ordinary life when God interrupted you. He gave you a new mission. Perhaps it was to pastor a church or work with the poor or minister to troubled teens. You might've thought you were unworthy because of your past mistakes and sins, but once you said, "Yes," to God's leading, you saw that God could use you in spite of your past—or maybe even because of it. God has a way of redeeming things like that.

Maybe you haven't had this experience yet. I can promise you it will come. God is a God of purpose, and He always gives you work to do. For now, you might still be in your Midian waiting for your new mission. Pray about it, keep your eyes open, and be ready to act.

You never know—it may happen while you're eating chicken soup for lunch.

Quest of the Day

1. Read Exodus 1-4.

2. Have you had your "burning bush" moment yet? Journal about it and share that story with a friend who needs some encouragement, whether that's in person, over e-mail, or on the phone, etc. Share it on social media with the hashtag #42Terraforming.

3. If you're not sure what your mission is, look up some ministries near you and volunteer with them. Do it

once or twice with each one to see which you like the most.

DAY 13: REFUSING CHANGE IN THE UNDISCOVERED COUNTRY
BY ERIC ANDERSON

"If my people, who are called by my name, will humble
themselves and pray…then I will hear from Heaven and
forgive their sins and heal their land."
2 Chronicles 7:14

Star Trek: The Undiscovered Country finds Captain Kirk at
a meeting with many high-level captains and officers. This is a
big deal, and Kirk wonders what is happening. Long story
short, the Klingons have only 50 years of life left because their
moon, Praxis, has exploded. Their only hope is to get help
from the Federation, but for that to happen, a peace must to
be brokered. Kirk isn't happy, especially when told he'd be
escorting the Klingon Chancellor, Gorkon, to the peace
meeting. During the journey, the Enterprise fires on the
Chancellor's ship. Gorkon is killed, and Kirk and McCoy are
quickly blamed and sent to a wintry prison planet. In reality,
the Klingon General Chang, Romulan Ambassador Nanclus,
and even Federation Admiral Cartwright planned the attack as
part of a conspiracy to maintain the state of conflict. Kirk then
begins the long road of reconciliation with the Klingons.

Pharaoh hated the idea of change. He did not want to
lose millions of slaves. In Moses' first audience with him, God
turned his staff into a snake. So did each of the sorcerers of the
Pharaoh with their staffs. Then Moses' snake ate the

staff/snakes of Pharaoh's sorcerers. Apparently, that wasn't enough. As Moses repeatedly came and presented God's demands and warnings, Pharaoh kept saying no. God sent one plague, then another, then another. Pharaoh kept refusing to let the Israelites go. Over time, 10 plagues were sent on Egypt: Water was turned to blood, frogs overran the land, gnats swarmed them, flies poured into Pharaoh's palace and the rest of Egypt. Livestock died in great number, Egyptians received boils, hail rained down, locusts consumed the area, and then darkness spread. Each time the Israelites were free from this tragedy and Pharaoh would say, "Pray and ask God to take this away." Then he would once again refuse to let the people go. Finally, God did the unthinkable. He sent a plague that killed the firstborn children in each household that did not have the blood of a lamb on its door posts. Only then did Pharaoh relent. But still, he changed his mind and chase God's people after they left. This only led to his army being swallowed by the Red Sea.

We should be asking ourselves, when have I been like Pharaoh? Am I currently refusing a change God wants me to make? This is no small question. The workbook *Experiencing God* by Henry Blackaby takes 12 units of five daily lessons each to consider seven steps in, well, experiencing God. Step number five is this: "God's invitation for you to work with him always leads you to a crisis of belief that requires faith and action."

We have this idea in some American church circles that following God makes everything fun and never requires you to do anything you do not want to do. This is not always the case. Although I believe that following Jesus will be adventurous, there are times when we are called to difficult tasks. I did not enjoy life in high school. In college I did not want to be around youth at all, and I purposely decided not to seek out jobs as a youth pastor. Now I'm a substitute teacher that works in high schools. I needed shaping by God needed to get me to be comfortable around teens, but He won. I am not sure how many things I missed because of my earlier misgivings and refusals.

Pharaoh hardened his heart when Moses asked him to change. Here is the thing: either way, if we agree to or refuse change, God still moves. He still accomplishes His goals and ends with or without us.

Quest of the Day

1. Read Exodus chapters 7-11.
2. How do you do with change? Do you like it or hate it?
3. How can you embrace change?

DAY 14: EXODUS FROM THE PLANET OF THE APES
BY NATHAN MARCHAND

Moses answered the people, "Do not be afraid. Stand firm
and you will see the deliverance the Lord will bring you
today. The Egyptians you see today you will never
see again. The Lord will fight for you; you need only to be
still."
Exodus 14:13-14

"Apes together strong!"

So declares Caesar, the leader of a tribe of intelligent
simians in *War for the Planet of the Apes*, the third entry in the
rebooted *Planet of the Apes* trilogy. By this point, Caesar has led
a revolution as a plague ravaged humanity. The virus kills
humans while enhancing the intelligence of apes. Many battles
followed, but by this film, Caesar protects his tribe from a
military organization called Alpha-Omega led by a ruthless
soldier known as the Colonel, who leads an attack on the apes'
home, killing Caesar's wife and eldest son.

The next day, the tribe prepares to journey to a new
home far away. Wanting to help himself and his people, Caesar
leaves to seek vengeance on the Colonel and act as a decoy.
Caesar is accompanied by his friends Maurice the orangutan,
Luca the gorilla, and Rocket the chimpanzee. Once they reach
the Alpha-Omega camp, Caesar discovers that the Colonel has
captured and enslaved his tribe. He is using them to build a

wall to protect his compound from other military forces. Unfortunately, Caesar is captured by a traitorous ape and joins his tribe in their slavery.

The Colonel confronts Caesar, telling him the virus has mutated, making the surviving humans devolve in primitive mutes. His campaign against the apes is to prevent the spread of this disease and save what few humans are left. Later, Caesar and Rocket concoct a plan to escape the facility via underground passages. They succeed, but Caesar remains behind to confront the Colonel. Ironically, when he finds his nemesis, he discovers he has been infected with the virus thanks to a ragdoll he confiscated from Caesar that belonged to a mute girl. Caesar watches as the Colonel commits suicide.

In the film's final moments, the apes cross a desert and arrive at an oasis. As Caesar and Maurice watch their tribe celebrate, the orangutan discovers the wound Caesar suffered in their escape is fatal. "Do not worry, Maurice," he tells his old friend. "You are home now. Apes are strong...with or without me." Then, after years of communicating only in sign language, Maurice speaks: "Son will know who was father...and what Caesar did for us."

For the past few days, we've been looking at the story of Moses. We've seen him receive his mission from God— liberate Israel from Egypt—and confront the hard-hearted

Pharaoh. Now we come to the most famous and epic part of his story: the Exodus.

After the Angel of Death slew the firstborns of Egypt, including Pharaoh's own son, the Israelites departed to journey to the Promised Land with Moses as their leader. But despite the devastation of the plagues, Pharaoh's heart once more turned against Israel, and he dispatched his armies to bring them back. God, who led His people by a pillar of smoke in the day and a pillar of fire by night, brought them to the Red Sea. Now the people found themselves trapped between the water and the Egyptian army. They lost heart, but Moses assured them that God himself would fight for them. And man, did He! Remember that classic scene in *The Ten Commandments* where God parts the Red Sea to allow the people to walk through on dry land and then drowns the Egyptians when they try to cross? It's all recorded in Exodus 14.

But even with that dramatic rescue, their journey would be a long one. Because of the people's disbelief, it would be 40 years before they reached the Promised Land. Moses, now an old man, climbed a mountain to see his people's new home from a distance, but he was not allowed to enter because of grievous sins he committed during the journey. He died and was buried by God on that mountain, the mantle of leadership passing to Joshua. Deuteronomy 34 closes with these words:

> Since then, no prophet has risen in Israel like Moses, whom the Lord knew face to face, who did all those signs and wonders the Lord sent him to do in Egypt—to Pharaoh and to all his officials and to his whole land. For no one has ever shown the mighty power or performed the awesome deeds that Moses did in the sight of all Israel (v. 10-12).

Sounds an awful lot like the ending of this film trilogy, doesn't it? The final entry in particular is replete with parallels to the Exodus. Like Moses, Caesar was the reluctant leader of his people. He liberated them from slavery. The Colonel was a hard-hearted foe destroyed by his own folly. And finally, Caesar died after seeing his people enter their new home from a distance, his best friend promising to make sure his story is remembered forever.

Do you find yourself "enslaved" to your own personal "Egypt" or stuck between an army and the Red Sea, so to speak? Take heart in knowing that God can liberate you! It may seem hopeless, but I can tell you from personal experience it is in the darkest moments that God shows up and surprise you. I can't tell you when or how it will happen, but it will happen. Look back on your life, and you'll probably recall times when God saved you. Hold onto those stories. They will give you hope no matter how dire the situation looks.

Quest of the Day

1. Read Exodus 13:17-14:31 and Deuteronomy 34.

2. How has God saved you in the past? What impossible situation did He liberate you from? Journal about that and put a copy of that story somewhere where you'll see it every day (on your desk, on your fridge, etc.) as a reminder of what He's done for you.

3. Are experiencing a "Red Sea moment"? I highly recommend reading the book *The Red Sea Rules* by Robert Morgan. It gives ten great lessons on what to do when you find yourself relying on God to save you in impossible situations.

DAY 15: RAPHAEL, GOD'S WAYS, AND THE PROMISED LAND
BY ERIC ANDERSON

...when you and your children return to the Lord your God and obey him with all your heart and with all your soul according to everything I have commanded you today, then the Lord your God will restore your fortunes....
Deuteronomy 30:2-3

Raphael is always a hothead. The other Teenage Mutant Ninja Turtles were used to him getting angry, going off on his own, and doing whatever. But one day this goes badly for them. They just started their rivalry with the Foot Clan, as seen in the first TMNT movie from 1990. Raphael got angry after arguing with Leonardo and goes to the roof. Then the Foot Clan attacks. In the fight, Raphael is seriously injured. They retreat to a farmhouse outside the city and wait there. In that time Leonardo never leaves Raphael's side. The whole group is out of sorts during this painful wait.

Defeat! After the victory of Jericho, Joshua and his army were humiliated. At Jericho they marched around the city for seven days before God miraculously destroyed the walls around the city. But now they failed to take the city of Ai. The story can be found in Joshua 7. Joshua sent about 3,000 of his army to take this small town, but they were routed by a small group of people and 36 were killed. "At this the hearts of the people melted in fear and became like water" (Joshua 7:5). As

Joshua prayed, God said this: "Israel has sinned; they have violated my covenant, which I commanded them to keep. They have taken some of the devoted things; they have stolen, they have lied, they have put them with their own possessions" (Joshua 7:11).

As Joshua had the people come forward, tribe by tribe, clan by clan, family by family, he found one person, Achan, who admitted to stealing silver, a robe, and a gold bar. Yes, one person, one member of the community, had been selfish and acted rashly…and other people were affected by this sin.

God expects all of His people to act in accordance with His ethics. He gave Israel a large goal and was so excited to give them aid. Yet when they wanted to do things their own ways, He was not happy. He would not allow His people to act selfishly.

When God calls you to something, He cares about the way you treat people as you go about the new mission and whether you are doing it with Him or trying to do it on your own. Achan got greedy and put his desires above the mission God had for them. Raphael got angry and ran from the team at a time when it was dangerous for all of them. This made it easier for the Foot Clan to pick him out and get him out of the way early in their attack. Did you notice that when Achan sinned, God held the whole community responsible? Our choices for how to chase God's new ideas for us must fit to

His ethics. This means sacrificing our own desires for Him, for those around us, and even for our own benefit.

Raphael always wants to rush right into situations, but often God wants us to wait for His timing. This can be frustrating, but remember it is His mission, not ours. He sees the issues we do not see and when we act selfishly and try do it our own way it does not sit well with Him.

Quest of the Day

1. Read Joshua 7-8.
2. Do you need to make amends with someone or a community due to a poor choice?

Day 16: Prayer Day 2

For the last five days you've been reading about the most seminal moments in Israel's history. God used a reluctant hero like Moses to defy an empire and liberate His people, and eventually they entered and conquered the Promised Land. There were pitfalls along the way, but in the end God's will prevailed like it always does.

God wants to give you a mission just like He did for Moses. It may not be as epic, but it is just as vital to the Kingdom. So, today you'll be praying about finding your mission.

Remember the "burning bush moment" you journaled about on day 12? Review that story in prayer. Remind yourself of God's providence. Many Psalms begin with such remembrances.

Did you compile a list of ministries on day 12? Have you contacted any of them or worked with them yet? Either way, spend several moments in silent prayer asking God to help you decide which ministry He wants you to do. Don't be afraid to tell Him what you want to do—God often works through your own desires and gifting.

What are the "Red Seas" blocking you from these opportunities? Find the copy of the story you wrote of a past impossible liberation God has done for you from day 14. Ask

Him to pave the way for your new mission by parting that "Red Sea."

Is that "Red Sea" your own hard heart as discussed on day 13? Spend a few minutes asking God to reveal that to you. If you feel His conviction, repent.

DAY 17: THE RELUCTANCE OF GIDEON AND CAPTAIN N
BY ERIC ANDERSON

"For the Lord and for Gideon!"
Judges 7:20

"For the Lord and for Gideon!" Such was the battle cry that rang out in front of the Midian camp. Midian pillaged and raided Israel for years until Gideon accepted the call to fight them in a rather interesting story, which is found in Judges 6-8. Gideon was visited by the Angel of the Lord. Even with an honorable greeting, he was skeptical of this calling. "If this is really you, wait for me to come back with an offering." The Lord did wait and burned the offering with a touch of Gideon's staff. Again, Gideon wanted proof so he set out a fleece and asked God to have it full of dew in the morning but the ground around it dry. There was a bowl's worth of water in the fleece but the ground was indeed dry. Then Gideon asked God to reverse the test, which God did marvelously as before.

Gideon finally accepted the call. He raised an army of 32,000, but then God said, "This is too big. Send some home." So all but 10,000 left. Then God said, "No, still too big. Take them to drink water and keep those who lap like a dog." So that is what Gideon did, with 300 staying. Just 300 out of 32,000. (And the Spartans thought they were special).

How do you feel about reluctant heroes? Are you one? Kevin, better known to us as Captain N the Game Master, was such a person. In this '90s cartoon, Kevin gets sucked into his NES to save Videoland from the tyranny of Mother Brain. Videoland consists of the various worlds from many Nintendo games. His team consists of Kid Icarus, Simon Belmont, Mega Man, Princess Lana, and his dog Duke. Upon his arrival, he doesn't want to stay. He thinks this is all bonkers and just wants to get back home. Then the Eggplant Wizard and King Hippo kidnap Princess Lana for Mother Brain. Captain N runs into action and almost saves her, but of course they get away so he has to convince the others to work together. After arguing about the way to get there, they do as a team rescue Princess Lana. At the end of the first episode he realizes he can stay and protect Videoland, or he can go home and do chores. He opts to stay with the Princess.

I think we all, at some point, get a calling that we don't feel is a good fit for us. Gideon had a lot of arguments for why he should not lead the army. This wasn't just humility; it was a denial of what God could do through him. He claimed God could not be with him for many reasons: the lack of miraculous wonders, his small stature among the Israelites, etc. What does God say?

"Go, in the strength you have and save Israel out of Midian's hands. Am I not sending you? ...I will be with you and you will strike down the Midianites" (Judges 6:14-16).

When God calls you to something, He will provide the power. There is a cliché out there that says, "God does not call the qualified but instead qualifies the called." It might be cheesy, but it is true in many ways. Why did God have Gideon send many soldiers away? So that He would shine. God tells Gideon, "You have too many men. I cannot deliver Midian into your hands or Israel would boast against me, 'My own strength has saved me'" (Judges 7:2). In other words, God would not get the glory, and Israel would just get a big head.

God did give the Midianites into Gideon's hand. The Kings of Midian and two high officials were killed in the battle and Israel was saved. They then asked Gideon to be their leader. Is God calling you to something you are reluctant to do? If yes, start asking God to give you courage and wisdom for the calling. Then, find a step to take into that calling.

<u>Quest of the Day</u>

1. Read Judges 6-8.
2. Do you ever want God to give a lot of help from others when He just wants to use you?
3. How can you cooperate with God in His work around you?

DAY 18: MALCOLM REYNOLDS' WIDOW
BY NATHAN MARCHAND

After this he loved a woman in the Valley of Sorek, whose
name was Delilah. And the lords of the Philistines came up to
her and said to her, "Seduce him, and see where his great
strength lies, and by what means we may overpower him, that
we may bind him to humble him. And we will each give you
1,100 pieces of silver."
Judges 16:4-5

Captain Malcolm Reynolds once learned a very
valuable lesson: never get drunk and dance with a pretty girl on
a backwater world. Why? You'll end up married to her.

No, the Serenity's crew wasn't vacationing in Las
Vegas in the *Firefly* episode "Our Mrs. Reynolds." They scare
off bandits for a town on a colony world, so in gratitude the
highly-religious townsfolk throw them a celebration. Mal is
enjoying himself some good booze when a cute little redhead
offers him a cup of wine and invites him to join her among the
jubilant dancers. The next day, hungover and in a hurry to meet
their next client, he and his crew depart only to discover they
had a stowaway—the little redhead.

When questioned on why she is there, she says she and
Mal are married. Apparently, her actions at the celebration
were something of a marriage custom. She claims she did this
to escape a harsh slave owner. Mal, unwilling to accept this,
declares they'll drop her off at the nearest colony where she

can find work. Meanwhile, he endures constant teasing from his shipmates. Shepherd Book warns him not to take sexual advantage of the girl by telling him there's a "special place in Hell. One they reserved for child molesters and people who talk at the theater." To say this makes Mal nervous would be the biggest understatement this side of the Black.

The girl, who says her name is Saffron, proceeds to wait on Mal like a demure and dutiful wife. She makes dinner for him. She offers to wash his feet. Despite the awkwardness this creates, Mal treats her well and encourages her to stand up for herself. He even refuses an offer from big dumb Jayne to trade his favorite gun for her. Finally, Mal goes to his quarters and finds Saffron, clothed only in a sheet, warming his bed. She says she wants to have her "wedding night," and despite contemplating that "special Hell," he succumbs to her kiss— and then succumbs to unconsciousness.

The crew resuscitates Mal and learns he was taken out by poison lipstick. The ship's course was set to take them to a "carrion house," an energy net that disassembles ships. Thanks to some quick thinking and Jayne's huge gun, "Vera," they manage to escape. Mal tracks Saffron to a snowy planet, where he confronts her by putting his gun to her head. He asks why she went to such trouble with her con game, and she replies, "You're assuming the payoff is the point." Mal asks what her real name is, and after replying with silence, he knocks her out, unsatisfied.

A similar story plays out in Judges 16. Samson, a Nazarite judge, is imbued by God with superhuman strength. He could kill a lion with his bare hands and slay a thousand Philistines with a donkey's jawbone—but he couldn't fight feminine wiles. He meets Delilah, a woman from the Valley of Sorek, and falls in love with her. Sadly, she betrays him when Philistines bribe her to learn the secret of his strength so that they may overpower and subdue him.

Three times she asks him. Three times he lies, telling her that if anyone did this or that to him, "I'll become as weak as any other man." Each time she tries these methods while he's sleeping and calls, "The Philistines are upon you!" but he remains strong. Each time she complains that he is making a fool of her, even going so far as to say he doesn't love her. Samson finally succumbs and tells her the truth: "No razor has ever been used on my head because I have been a Nazirite dedicated to God from my mother's womb. If my head were shaved, my strength would leave me, and I would become as weak as any other man" (Judges 16:17).

With that, she rests his head in her lap and shaves his head while he sleeps. When Samson wakes, he is accosted by his enemies. The Philistines gouge out his eyes and make him a slave. But God was gracious to His imperfect servant—

Samson's hair grew back. Then during a religious festival, he was brought out by the Philistines to be mocked, and after a short prayer, God granted Samson his strength one last time. He dislodged the support pillars holding up the temple, and it collapsed, killing them all.

Do you find yourself in a situation like Mal or Samson? Have you been working hard at the tasks God has given you only to be undone by your sins? Perhaps you started off strong, but sin crept in. Not just one or two sins, but persistent, unrepentant sins. Maybe it was lying. Maybe it was porn. Maybe it was stealing. You justified them to yourself. "It's only a peek." "It's just a white lie." "No one will notice a little missing money." What you didn't realize was this vice was slowly eroding away at the strengths God gave you. Eventually, it caught up with you. Whatever your Saffron or Delilah was, you were ousted. It cost you your job, your friends, your marriage. Everything. Maybe you even went to jail because of it.

I'm here to tell you there is still hope. If you repent, God will grant you new strength. You may not be as mighty as you once were or overcome all the consequences of your sins, but He will empower you to serve Him again. It will take time (remember, Samson's hair had to regrow), and it won't be easy, but it will happen. God has a long history of using "broken saints" to accomplish great tasks. There's comfort in knowing that if He can use someone like Samson, He can use you.

<u>Quests of the Day</u>

1. Read Judges 16.

2. What are the "Saffrons" and "Delilahs" in your life? The sins you allowed to define your lifestyle? Write them down. Be honest.

3. Pray through that list, asking God for forgiveness. When you're finished, tear up that list and throw it away. Better yet, burn it. This will be a symbol of you renouncing these sins and dedicating yourself to avoiding them in the future with God's help.

Day 19: True Love Breaks the Curse
By Eric Anderson

A friend loves at all times, and a brother is born for a time of
adversity.
Proverbs 17:17

The book of Ruth is a romance. It's the story of a
Moabite woman who lost her husband and chose to stay with
her Hebrew mother-in-law, Naomi, instead of going home.
She met a man named Boaz, who met her material needs and
then her relational need.

Many guys would say that I should identify as Boaz. As
a man I should be focused on supporting and caring for the
lady. But I don't identify with Boaz. I don't see myself as a
provider. I have no problem paying for a date, but I am not the
natural socialite I want to be. I tend to identify with Ruth for a
couple reasons. She was loyal to a fault, and I tend to be as
well. She was a foreigner in a land not her own, and I often feel
that way. I "fall through the cracks" socially.

In Disney movies I resonate with Aladdin but also with
the Beast. Both of them are in some way out of sorts with the
society around them, but they deal with it very differently.
Aladdin takes to the streets alone (aside from his pet monkey,
Abu) and tries to care for himself by stealing from others and
is constantly surrounded by cruel palace guards out to arrest

him. He has to steal food as he does not have a job and gets into fights quite often. The Beast is more of a recluse. He is paying for a terrible choice and stays locked away in a castle because social interaction is hard for him after the curse was thrust upon him. He refused to help an old woman but offered shelter to a young lady who turned out to be an Enchantress. For his lack of hospitality, she cursed him into the form of a beast.

Ruth, Aladdin, and the Beast all have something in common. They all have two relationships that are very important in their stories. One person helps them. This person is a mentor, a best friend, even a trainer. The Beast has a team of servants, but Cogsworth and Lemiere stand out. They give him advice and lead the other servants in preparing events for Belle and the Beast. Aladdin has the Genie, who gives him a whole new life. They then meet someone who meets an emotional need. Aladdin meets Princess Jasmine and fakes a new identity to woo her. Belle comes to Beast's castle to find her dad, and he makes her stay. Through her, he learns how to love.

Ruth had a more unique story. At first, Naomi tried to send her away. This worked with the other daughter-in-law, but not so much with Ruth. Ruth stood her ground and refused to leave. She vowed that Naomi's god was her god and Naomi's people were her people. She would not leave Naomi alone. They went back to Judah, and Ruth was everyone knew her because she stood out as a foreigner. While gleaning, she met Boaz. This older gentleman was a provider, but more than that, he was a kinsman-redeemer (a male relative who acts on behalf of a family member in trouble or in need), which meant he was expected to aid anyone in Naomi's family caught in difficult situations (Deuteronomy 25 and Leviticus 25). He made sure Ruth was safe while gleaning. Then came the advice from Naomi. Can you imagine your mother-in-law giving you dating advice? Awkward. But in this case it was a lifesaver. Ruth followed Naomi's instructions and approached Boaz at work. He bought the field owned by Naomi's dead husband and married Ruth. This provided for both Ruth and Naomi.

Here is the kicker: we all want another person to be our Boaz or we want to be Boaz. Sometimes both conditions are true. You want to provide, but you also want someone to provide for you. Are you open to a new relationship to help you or for you to help someone else? God does work through people, and we see it again and again in how God will bring a new person to a situation to change it. You have to ready when that person is you. Sometimes you'll be Naomi, someone who gives advice to another or provide for someone in some sort of relational way or with physical needs.

There is the point where you must unlearn what you have learned: Jesus is Boaz. He is the ultimate redeemer who saves us when we are "poor in spirit" (Matthew 5:3). In reality we all have times when we are Ruth, a person in great need. He died a painful death on the cross to forgive us our sins and cleanse us of all unrighteousness. He protects us when we are gleaning. He provides extra to fill our needs. He brings us to people who will walk with us through all of life.

<u>Quest of the Day:</u>

1. Read the book of Ruth.

2. Write down what you learn from it or share it with someone.

3. Write down the names of three of people who have needs—whether material, emotional, or social—that you can meet. Set time aside this week to do that.

Day 20: The Green Goliath
by Nathan Marchand

"Your servant has killed both the lion and the bear; this
uncircumcised Philistine will be like one of them, because he
has defied the armies of the living God. The Lord who
rescued me from the paw of the lion and the paw of the bear
will rescue me from the hand of this Philistine."
-1 Samuel 17:36-37

Heroscape is the best board game ever. Of all time. (Kudos to you if you got that reference).

A few years ago, Eric invited me and a bunch of his friends to his house for a weekend of gaming. He had so many Heroscape sets that he created a massive board that covered the entire living room floor. There were mountains, lakes, lava, swamps, trees, rocks—you name it, it was there. Eric decided that each of the eight players could select a character from the Marvel Master Set as their general and build a team around him. I chose Captain America and gave him a team of World War II commandos consisting of Sgt. Drake Alexander (who has a bionic arm and a katana) and the Airborne Elite (paratroopers). And yes, it was awesome.

On my first turn, I deployed the Airborne Elite into a castle in the middle of the huge board. For the most part, they just sat there twiddling their thumbs. Meanwhile, Cap and Drake were kicking butt and taking names. Alas, even they could not stave off the hoards around them. When the dust settled, all that remained were my Airborne Elite in their little fortress and mine and Eric's mutual friend Henry, whose army consisted of a heavily-damaged Hulk and some Vikings. As you'd expect, the lower the Hulk's health, the higher his attack power. I had every reason to be afraid.

Henry, who was having the best Heroscape game he'd ever played, rushed the Hulk and his Vikings at the castle. I managed to snipe the Vikings thanks to the Airborne Elite's excellent attack range. I even scored a hit on the Hulk, taking him down to one HP. By that point, though, the Not-So-Jolly Green Giant was standing at the castle door, ready to break it down. I had the biggest of barbarians at my gate. So, with certain defeat imminent, I decided to use the Elite's Grenade Special Attack just for fun. Henry laughed at me. He was rolling eight or ten dice against my two. We rolled our "chance cubes," and I hoped the proverbial "dice gods" favored me.

I scored one hit. Everyone's jaws dropped. The impossible had happened. Victory was mine.

The Bible records another epic underdog battle in 1 Samuel 17: the famous story of David and Goliath. David, a shepherd boy who anointed king by the prophet Samuel, delivered food to his brothers, who were fighting in Israel's army against the Philistines. When he arrived, he learned that the nearly ten-foot-tall Philistine champion, Goliath, had been mocking the Israelite army for 40 days. "Choose a man and have him come down to me," said the defiant giant. "If he is able to fight and kill me, we will become your subjects; but if I overcome him and kill him, you will become our subjects and serve us." But no Israelite had the courage to take Goliath's challenge.

Except David.

King Saul told David he was crazy, saying, "You are only a boy, and [Goliath] has been a fighting man since his youth" (1 Sam. 17:33b). David replied by saying he had killed lions and bears while protecting his father's flocks and that Goliath would be no different. "The Lord who delivered me from the paw of the lion and the paw of the bear will deliver me from the hand of this Philistine" (1 Sam. 17:37). Although David's trust was ironclad, Saul did try to give the teenage boy armor, but it was too heavy. Instead, David went to a stream and selected five sooth stones.

What followed became one of the seminal moments in Israel's history. David confronted the giant, imbedding a stone in Goliath's forehead with his sling. He then decapitated his foe with his own sword (can you say, "FATALITY"?). Their champion dead, the rest of the Philistines were routed by the Israelites.

God did a mighty new thing in Israel's history because David trusted in Him for deliverance. Though he was skilled and performed incredible feats, he attributed those accomplishments to God. It was the Lord, not him, who had slain the lion and the bear. And it was these past experiences that gave David the confidence that God would do the same for him against Goliath. Because of this, a humble shepherd boy killed a giant.

Perhaps you're facing your own "Green Goliath," as Stan Lee sometimes called the Hulk. Debt that keeps piling up. A nasty boss at work. A day in court. Whatever it is, think back on the times when God has delivered you. It doesn't matter if it was big or small. Those were your lions, your bears. They were preparing you for this much bigger challenge. Things don't have to stay the same. God is more than capable of bringing change, of doing something new. Either your circumstances will change, or you'll change to endure your challenges. Step out in faith. Do your part. Leave the rest to God.

And watch your giants fall.

<u>Quests of the Day</u>

1. Read 1 Samuel 17.

2. What is a big challenge you'll soon be facing? Write down what it is and why it worries you. Then think back on how God has delivered you in the past. Remembering these things reminds us God is trustworthy.

3. In light of this, what can you do to prepare for this challenge? I recommend reading *Goliath Must Fall* Louis Giglio as part of your preparation.

Day 21: An Extreme Meekness
By Eric Anderson

"But I tell you, love your enemies and pray for those who
persecute you."
Matthew 5:44

Kenshin Himura, a travelling swordsman, settles down
at a dojo to help Kaoru, the Assistant Master of the Kamiya
Kasshin style. Kenshin is known as the dangerous warrior
Battousai the Manslayer, but he is a gentle and humble man
who has vowed never to kill again. One of his many battles is
against Sojiro Seta, an unemotional young boy who is just as
strong as Kenshin. This boy is the second-in-command for a
group called the Juppongatana. The second fight between
them takes up several episodes of *Rurouni Kenshin*. Two
opposing viewpoints were at war here.

"If you're strong you live, if you're weak you die."

"I will protect the weak and never kill again."

Kenishin, a powerful warrior feared throughout Japan,
at the moment when he could end Sojiro, holds his blade.
Sojiro stares in confusion. "Do you think you can defeat me
without killing me?" he asks. Kenshin could have killed him at
the height of the battle, but he chose not to do it. His vow
against killing was far more important than any vendetta. He
senses that something else is at work in Sojiro, who then

remembers his first kill. He recalls smiling but also crying. He did not want to be a killer. Kenshin, who has this knack for pointing people toward redemption, moves Sojiro in a new direction. The boy realizes he does not have to keep the law of strength he was taught. He moves on and looks for something new.

Kenshin exemplifies meekness. Meekness is a control of your power. In *Jurassic Park*, Doctor Ian Malcolm is famous for saying of scientists, "They were so preoccupied with whether or not they could, they didn't stop to think if they should." That is what meekness seeks to prevent. It means stopping and asking God, "Should I do this?" It is not in any way weakness, which is a lack of power, but it is a control of the power one holds. This self-control is expected to be held in submission to Christ.

David is famous for two occasions of meekness. In one event found in 1 Samuel 24, he was being hunted by King Saul. Saul came into a cave to relieve himself when David and his men were hiding in it. His men urged him to go kill Saul where he stood. David crept up, cut a piece of Saul's robe off, and moved back. He was actually conscience-stricken for even doing that much. Later, when Saul exited the cave, David called down to him:

> "Then David went out of the cave and called out to Saul, "My lord the king!" When Saul looked behind him, David

bowed down and prostrated himself with his face to the ground. He said to Saul, "Why do you listen when men say, 'David is bent on harming you'? This day you have seen with your own eyes how the Lord delivered you into my hands in the cave. Some urged me to kill you, but I spared you; I said, 'I will not lay my hand on my lord, because he is the Lord's anointed" (1 Samuel 24:8-9).

David held Saul in a high respect. He saw him as one of the Lord's anointed because, quite frankly, he was. The fact that this King had rebelled and God had chosen to replace him did not change the respect David was expected to give him.

Jesus also showed great meekness. While being accused in front of Pilate, Jesus stayed silent. He did not try to defend Himself because there was a bigger plan at work. Before that, while being arrested, he told Peter, "Don't you think I could call down a legion of angels to stop them?" Instead, Jesus allowed Himself to be arrested, put on trial with many false accusations, tortured, and given a form of death so painful they created a new word from which we get the English word "excruciating." Jesus meekly took our sin upon Himself to provide freedom from sin and redemption for us all. We just need to admit our sin and accept His gift.

You have enormous power from God. You will be tempted to use your power harshly, but do not do this. Submit your power to God. You have a voice in this world. You will want to lash out at people, but do not do this. Control your tongue with Christ's help. You have a drive for victory. You will want to seek revenge, but do not do this. Let God be your vindicator.

<u>Quest of the Day</u>

1. Read 1 Samuel 24.
2. Read Matthew 27:11-26.

DAY 22: PRAYER DAY 3 - PRAYING THE PSALMS

Today's prayer day is a little different. You'll be using the Psalms, which are essentially poetic prayers set to music. It's appropriate since many of them were written by David, and you've been reading about him the past few days. It's good to read these songs aloud while praying and claim the words as your own. Do it slowly, though, so you can meditate on the words and let them sink in. It'd be a good idea to select a few to memorize. Psalm 23 would be a good one to start with since it's short and well-known.

Here are a few verses from some Psalms that tie in with some recent entries. We recommend reading each one in their entirety today.

Day 19: New Relationships – Psalm 68

Sing to God, sing in praise of his name,

extol him who rides on the cloud;

rejoice before him—his name is the LORD.

A father to the fatherless, a defender of widows,

is God in his holy dwelling.

God sets the lonely in families,

he leads out the prisoners with singing;

but the rebellious live in a sun-scorched land (v. 4-6)

Day 20: Newness in Trust – Psalm 27

The Lord is my light and my salvation—

whom shall I fear?

The Lord is the stronghold of my life—

of whom shall I be afraid?

When the wicked advance against me

to devour me,

it is my enemies and my foes

who will stumble and fall.

Though an army besiege me,

my heart will not fear;

though war break out against me,

even then I will be confident. (v. 1-3)

Day 21: David's Prayer for Salvation from Saul –

Psalm 57

Have mercy on me, my God, have mercy on me,

for in you I take refuge.

I will take refuge in the shadow of your wings

until the disaster has passed.

I cry out to God Most High,

to God, who vindicates me.

He sends from heaven and saves me,

rebuking those who hotly pursue me—

God sends forth his love and his faithfulness. (v. 1-3)

DAY 23: JOSIAH AND THE MARTIAN MANHUNTER
BY ERIC ANDERSON

Blessed are those who find wisdom, who gain
understanding....
Proverbs 3:13

We tend to hate old ideas. We think that recent ideas
are the only source of newness. They certainly are not the only
source. Many claim that the Bible is "old hat" or "outdated."
But some things that are "outdated" are more powerful than
any new idea.

In the double episode arc of the *Justice League* animated
series called "Hearts and Minds," John Stewart walks into
trouble. He is on a planet called Kalanor, and a tyrant named
Desperot is in control. He has plans to send his armies,
powered by the Flame of Py'tar, to conquer planets and add
more millions to his cult. Several members of the Justice
League come to help in this fight, including Martian
Manhunter (J'onn J'onzz). He notices some writing, and while
asking about it, he finds that nobody there can read it. As the
team works with the local rebellion, they find the only way to
stop Desperot was to build a carbon bomb to take out the
source of his power, the Flame of Py'tar. In the middle of this,
the Martian Manhunter goes with the team to deliver the bomb
but stops them. Using his telepathy, he communes with the

Flame itself, and he hears an old story that radically changes the situation. The Flame of Py'tar was never meant to conquer. It was meant to turn the planet from a desert into a luscious, green jungle planet. Its power is meant to provide for people, not to enslave anyone. An old truth, written out for them, had been ignored, and that ignorance led to pain and suffering.

King Josiah was very familiar with this issue of idolatry. He tore down many idols and had the Temple in Jerusalem remodeled for the work of ministry. While getting money out of the treasury to pay for this work, Hilkiah the priest found the Book of the Law. This was the book written by Moses, also known as the Pentateuch, which included Genesis, Exodus, Leviticus, Numbers, and Deuteronomy. They seem to have not been studying it or using it in ministry. As Shaphan the secretary read the book to the King, Josiah's heart broke as he realized how the Law of God had been violated over and over, especially by the kings who came before him. He tore his robes in pain and depression. He sent a delegation to "inquire of the Lord." They went to a prophetess who had some hard news and some good news. Part of the hard news was that the curses and warnings listed for sin would still come to pass in the future. But there was still mercy from God.

"Tell the king of Judah...This is what the Lord, the God of Israel says, concerning the words you heard: Because your heart was responsive and you humbled yourself before God

83

when you heard what he spoke against this place and its
people, and because you humbled yourself before me and
tore your robes and wept in my presence, I have heard you,
declares the Lord...Your eyes will not see all the disaster I
am going to bring on this place and on those who live here"
(2 Chronicles 34:24-29).

Josiah gained time for his people. God would still bring the
difficult discipline that was promised, but Josiah had been
responsive to conviction, and this bought the people time to
repent.

Sometimes we need old truth to receive newness from
God. Perhaps you remember a time when you were depressed
and gained hope from Scripture. Maybe you have had a
Scripture show you your own sin and have sought repentance.
If you have not, keep reading. Keep studying the Scriptures.
Let Christ meet you in "outdated" ideas.

Quest of the Day

1. Read Josiah's story in 2 Chronicles 34 and 35.
2. How did seeking God terraform Josiah's heart?
3. How did it allow him to terraform his nation?

DAY 24: MOVE LIKE A BUTTERFLY, FAIL ON THE WII
BY NATHAN MARCHAND

So they shouted louder and slashed themselves with swords
and spears, as was their custom, until their blood
flowed. Midday passed, and they continued their frantic
prophesying until the time for the evening sacrifice. But there
was no response, no one answered, no one paid attention.
1 Kings 18:28-29

If you only played Wii Sports with your grandparents
at the old folks' home, you might've not known there was more
than bowling on it. The game also had baseball, tennis, and
golf. My favorite, though, was boxing. It was the only game
that required the use of the nunchuk (an accessory that
attached to the Wii-mote, making it look like Bruce Lee's
trademark weapon). You'd hold the Wii-mote and nunchuk in
each hand and then swing your hands to simulate throwing
punches.

I had a long, sometimes unfriendly gaming rivalry with
my younger brother Josiah when we were growing up. There
came a point when he exceeded me as a gamer. It didn't matter
what the game was: *Street Fighter II*, *Halo*, *Guitar Hero*—video
games just came easy to him. I guess you could say he was "The
Wizard" (though he didn't need a Power Glove).

We had an epic session of Wii Boxing one evening. He
sat on his bed, relaxing, while I was jumping around doing my

best Muhammad Ali impersonation to psyche myself up. For the next hour, I threw punches, bellowed war cries, and fell on the floor after each round. Sweat glistened on my face and darkened whatever nerdy shirt I was wearing. Meanwhile, Josiah just sat on his bed and flicked his wrists to throw his punches. He snickered at my melodramatic frustration. I wanted to win once. Just once. But I never won a single round. I came close a few times, but Josiah always took me down with some well-placed blows. I may have moved like a butterfly, but Josiah swatted me every time.

First Kings 18 tells of an equally humorous and one-sided contest. The prophet Elijah went to the wicked King Ahab and Queen Jezebel and chastised them for abandoning the Lord and serving Baal, in turn leading Israel to do the same. The king and queen wouldn't waver, and the people said nothing. So, he issued a challenge: gather the 450 prophets of Baal to meet him at Mount Carmel. Get two bulls, one for him and one for them, and prepare them for sacrifice. They would then pray to their respective gods, and whichever one answered by fire (i.e. burned the sacrifice), he was the true god Israel would serve.

Can you imagine Elijah, the Baal prophets, and the people gathering on Mt. Carmel for this? It's too bad Michael Buffer wasn't around; he'd make it even more exciting. "In this corner, we have the 450 prophets of Baal. And in this corner we have Elijah, the last of the Lord's prophets. Let's get ready to *RUMBLE!*"

Anyway, the Baal prophets prayed and danced around the altar all morning, but their god didn't answer. They got so desperate, they started cutting themselves with blades in the hopes of getting Baal to respond. By noon Elijah started taunting them like he was a pro-wrestler recording a promo: "Shout louder! Surely he is a god! Perhaps he is deep in thought, or busy, or traveling. Maybe he is sleeping and must be awakened" (1 Kings 18:27). (The ESV translation of this verse is truly a low blow, saying Baal "is relieving himself"). After hours of misery, the prophets of Baal finally gave up.

Elijah, though, upped the ante when it was his turn. He built an altar out of stone and dug a trench around it. Then he told the people to pour big jars of water on the altar not once, not twice, but *thrice!* Water soaked the altar and filled the trench. It'd be like trying to start a fire in a grill full of water.

But that was exactly what Elijah wanted.

He prayed a simple prayer, saying, "Lord, the God of Abraham, Isaac and Israel, let it be known today that you are God in Israel and that I am your servant and have done all these things at your command. Answer me, Lord, answer me, so these people will know that you, Lord, are God, and that you are turning their hearts back again" (1 Kings 18:36-37).

Immediately, fire engulfed the altar and consumed the sacrifice. (I like to imagine a fireball fell from the sky, but I've seen too many fantasy movies). The people declared that the Lord was God, and Elijah executed the prophets of Baal.

What are the false gods and idols in your life? Idolatry doesn't have to be literal. It can be anything that replaces God. Is it your job? Your reputation? Your friends? It could be these or any number of other things you dedicate your time and energy to. Workaholics will run themselves ragged trying to climb the corporate ladder and/or make extra money. Some people, on the other hand, are obsessed with climbing a social ladder. Others bend over backwards to create a "perfect" public image on social media. In the end it's only metaphorical bloodletting that amounts to nothing. Like my Wii Boxing bouts with my brother and the Baal prophets' prayers, it's a fight you cannot win.

If you find yourself in this miserable state, it might take a dramatic display of God's power to wake you up. You might even have to hit rock bottom before you repent. God is your creator, your savior, your sustainer. He deserves to be the first priority in your life. Everything else, no matter how good, is secondary. To put your trust in anything else is foolish. It can never save you.

Make a change. Put down the Wii-mote and repent.

Quest of the Day

1. Read I Kings 18.

2. What are your priorities in life? Write them down. Be honest with yourself. Is serving God number one, or have you let other things replace Him?

3. Commit to starting your day with reading the Bible (perhaps in conjunction with this book), even if it means skipping or delaying your breakfast. Something as small as this can help you put God first. Maybe you could pray in the shower. What else is your mind doing then?

Day 25: The Succession of the Dread Prophet Elijah
By Eric Anderson

And the things you have heard me say in the presence of
many witnesses entrust to reliable people who will also be
qualified to teach others.
2 Timothy 2:2

All the prophets were aware of what was happening.
As Elijah and his prophet padawan, Elisha, walked to their
destination, the warning kept coming. "Do you know that your
master will be taken from over you today?" Elijah himself
warned Elisha to stop. Elisha kept vowing, "As the Lord lives
and as you live, I will not leave you." Everyone knew that
Elijah was being taken to Heaven that day. The two men had
been serving God together for a while, and Elisha had learned
a lot from Elijah.

In *The Princess Bride*, we find a man who has taken a
mantle with far less public notice. Westley recalls to Buttercup
how he became the Dread Pirate Roberts. After being captured
by the Pirate, he was often threatened, "Goodnight, Westley.
Good work. Sleep well. I'll most likely kill you in the morning."
This kept happening, but it "was a fine time" for Westley. He
learned fencing and sailing and "anything anyone would teach
me." Eventually the captain retired and offered the mantle of
leadership to Westley. This man had been the third in a line of

Dread Pirate Roberts, and the name itself was the real power, so it was continually passed down from one man to another.

Succession is a frequent part of life and leadership. Churches gain new pastors. Business people and politicians retire. Students slowly turn into teachers. Children become parents or uncles/aunts. You cannot become a leader without first being a follower.

Elijah anointed Elisha in a time of weariness. The story is found in 1 Kings 19. He was hiding in a cave at Mount Horeb depressed and weary from years of ministry work, and the pain of being hunted by evil rulers. Any pastor will tell you that ministry is hard enough without a threat upon your life, yet Elijah and some ministry leaders in certain nations and regions today have to deal with both. Elijah had had enough, and God took grace on him and gave him orders to find a protégé who could take some of the burden off him and then take the mantle up when time came.

When my brother was in high school, he and some others started a student Bible group, but the administration was slow in letting them start it. This wasn't illegal or unconstitutional as it was an optional, student-led group that did not interrupt educational times. Eventually they had to refuse to leave the principal's office to get themselves taken seriously. Later on I was on a team that worked to start one in the middle school with mentoring from adults. At that time a new group also started at the high school, so I continued there, and eventually I went to two other cities, still a junior in high school, to help with training. Now as a substitute teacher I go and I sit with the kids when they have their own meetings. They lead, and I'm just there to encourage or to be encouraged by them. All of this is affecting the same school and town over decades. Each group, my brothers, mine, and the current students', have all had different sets of challenges, but we are part of one interweaved pattern led by the Holy Spirit.

Are you living such a pattern anywhere? Are you receiving mentoring? Are you mentoring someone else? If not, who can you ask to come alongside you? You need a mentor to show you where you need to grow and to have assistance when life is difficult. Then you need to share that experience with someone else and to have assistance when life is difficult. Hopefully you don't have to kidnap them and threaten their life to keep them growing.

Quest of the Day

1. Read 2 Kings 2 where Elisha receives the mantle from Elijah.

2. Jesus mentored twelve men. Some of the training he gave them is shared in Matthew 10. Read that chapter.

3. Find someone and share what you learn from these passages with them or share it with your regular Bible

study group. You could also post about it on social media with the hashtag #42Terraforming.

Day 26: The Zero Sacrifice
by Nathan Marchand

Then he said to me, "Prophesy to the breath; prophesy,
son of man, and say to it, 'This is what the
Sovereign Lord says: Come, breath, from the four
winds and breathe into these slain, that they may live.'" So
I prophesied as he commanded me, and breath entered
them; they came to life and stood up on their feet—a vast
army.
Ezekiel 37:9-10

Imagine Rip Van Winkle as a super fighting robot. His name is X, the hero of the classic Super Nintendo game *Mega Man X*. His creator, Dr. Light, believed humanity wasn't ready for a robot as advanced as X, so he locked him away in suspended animation. A century later, he is discovered by a Reploid (sentient robot) named Zero during a war between rogue Reploids called Mavericks, under the leadership of the sinister Sigma, and humans. X reluctantly joins his new friend Zero as a Maverick Hunter.

On his first mission, X confronts a powerful Maverick named Vile piloting an armored carrier on a bridge. Vile beats X within an inch of his life, clutching him in his mech's hand.

From off-screen comes the sound of humming energy. A plasma blast flies in and severs the mech's arm. And in dashes Zero. Vile wisely retreats.

"I guess I'm not powerful enough to defeat him," laments X.

"You shouldn't expect to defeat him," Zero reassures him. "He is designed to be a war machine. Remember, you have not reached full power yet. If you use all the abilities you were designed with, you should become stronger. You may even become as powerful as I am." After telling X he'll scout ahead, he adds, "X, I know you can do it!"

And grow in power he does. As X battles Maverick generals, he discovers capsules left by Dr. Light. Each one gives him an upgrade: dash boots, body armor, the world's hardest hardhat. There is an upgraded cannon, but if the player wants to see the most poignant moment of the game, he must refrain from finding it.

X and Zero storm Sigma's fortress. They're confronted once more by Vile, who cages Zero in a stasis field. X fights Vile and his armored carrier. Again, the malevolent Maverick beats X within an inch of his life. Zero breaks out of his cage and jumps onto Vile's carrier—and self-destructs. When the dust settles, the carrier is gone but Vile is untouched. X suddenly finds a second wind. Vile is flabbergasted, but he says, "You are still too weak! Prepare to be terminated!" Famous last words. X destroys the, well, vile Vile.

His foe vanquished, X finds Zero on the floor, dying. He tells X, "You are more powerful than you were before, but

Sigma is much more than he appears to be. You're going to need an edge. Take my arm cannon and your attack power should increase. Good luck, X!" With that, Zero pulls an Obi-Wan and disintegrates.

In the Bible, the prophet Ezekiel received several strange visions from God (flying wheels, multi-eyed creatures). Chapter 37 is one that sounds like it belongs in a fantasy novel. God shows him a valley of dry bones and commands the prophet to say to them,

> "Dry bones, hear the word of the Lord! This is what the Sovereign Lord says to these bones: I will make breath enter you, and you will come to life. I will attach tendons to you and make flesh come upon you and cover you with skin; I will put breath in you, and you will come to life. Then you will know that I am the Lord" (Ezekiel 37:4b-6).

These words make the bones reconnect into bodies, tendons and flesh forming on them and skin covering them. Can you imagine seeing this happen? This macabre but astonishing miracle. I'd pay to see this recreated on film or in a video game.

These reformed bodies, though, were still dead, so God commanded Ezekiel to prophecy over them again by saying, "Prophesy to the breath; prophesy, son of man, and say to it, 'This is what the Sovereign Lord says: Come, breath, from the four winds and breathe into these slain, that they may live'"

(Ezekiel 37:9). With this, the spark of life returned to those bodies, and they arose as a mighty army.

God tells the prophet these bones are symbolic of Israel, His exiled people who had lost all hope of ever returning to their homeland. He gives Ezekiel another prophecy, but this one is for Israel:

> "My people, I am going to open your graves and bring you up from them; I will bring you back to the land of Israel. Then you, my people, will know that I am the Lord, when I open your graves and bring you up from them. I will put my Spirit in you and you will live, and I will settle you in your own land. Then you will know that I the Lord have spoken, and I have done it, declares the Lord" (Ezekiel 37:12-14).

With these words, the people were refreshed and reinvigorated. Their God hadn't forgotten them. Just like when they were slaves in Egypt, He heard their cries for restoration. His words would enter their hearts and resurrect their hope. Their exile would end and they would go home. (And eventually, as seen in 1948, they would become a nation once more).

Have you lost hope in your own "exile"? You may be in the midst of circumstances that seem to have trapped you. Any light you see at the end of the tunnel may as well be a freight train barreling toward you. You may even think God has abandoned you, and no pain is greater than feeling forsaken by God. Just ask David (Ps. 22:1) and Jesus (Matt. 27:46, Mark 15:34). If your "exile" was brought on by your own bad decisions, you might even believe you deserve to be abandoned, leaving you in a cage of self-condemnation. I know because I've been there many times.

But the words God spoke to Ezekiel apply just as much to you. Read them again. Let them sink into your soul. The Holy Spirit has an uncanny ability to make the words of Scripture jump out at people even if they've read them many times before. Your "exile" won't last forever. God hears you. He can bring you out of it. Let Him restore your hope. This isn't wishful thinking. Biblical hope is a firm belief that good things are in store for you. God is trustworthy and gracious.

So, whether you're a super fighting robot in need of re-energizing or a pile of bones waiting to be knit back together, let God's words restore your hope.

Quest of the Day

1. Read Ezekiel 37.
2. Write out the key verses of Ezekiel's prophecy on a 3x5 card and post it where you'll see it every day (mirror, refrigerator, door, etc.). Or, if you prefer, other verses along the same lines.
3. Read these every day for a week. Journal about how you feel each day. Do you feel more hopeful? Chronicle this restoration.

DAY 27: FOR SUCH A TIMELINE AS THIS
BY ERIC ANDERSON

...and let us run with perseverance the race marked out for
us.
Hebrews 12:1b

Esther is an amazing story. If you ever get the chance
to attend a Purim celebration, do so. The Jews have a
wonderful tradition of holding not just a puppet show to
celebrate what God did in the story of Esther, but they also
encourage crowd interaction. Attendees are expected to "boo"
for Haman and shout/clap/stomp for the heroes, but most of
all Mordecai. Mordechai was Esther's uncle who took care of
her. When King Xerxes needed a new wife, Esther was
brought into the harem and eventually chosen to be the new
queen. Haman was an official who wanted all the glory. He
grew angry at Mordecai when he refused to bow to him.
Haman was trying to manipulate the King into destroying all
Jews so Mordecai sought Esther's help in dealing with the
problem. He asked her to approach the King to ask him to
make a proclamation on behalf of the Jews. This was
dangerous. Approaching the King without being called by him
was illegal. If he was not happy with it, he could have her killed.
While convincing her to help, Mordechai said,

> "Do not think that because you are in the king's house you
> alone of all the Jews will escape. For if you remain silent at

this time, relief and deliverance for the Jews will arise from another place, but you and your father's family will perish. And who knows but that you have come to your royal position for such a time as this?" (Esther 4:13-14).

The heroes of the TV show *The Librarians* were put into place for "such a time as this." In the season one finale, "The Librarians and the Loom of Fate," Eva Baird finds herself moving from timeline to timeline because Dulaque messed with the Loom of Fate. In each one Flyn Carsen had not become the Librarian and a different LiT (Librarian in Training) was in his place. Each time they could not solve part of the equation, and each time there was an extreme and immediate danger. Jake doesn't know that the trees are not common to that region, which is important for the portal. Ezekiel doesn't know that they could use something like an electrical current to save the people. Cassandra is having a hard time saving the people from dragons. Finally, they pull all of them into one reality together, and they send Eva and Flynn back to the Loom to solve the problem and get everyone back into the original timeline. All of them are important to the story and the same reality. All of them have to cooperate to protect the artifacts and the Library.

Providential placement, fate, destiny. Different terms for a very specific idea. God has plans. He has purposes. He often invites us into those plans and purposes. You do have a choice, but as Mordicai tells Esther, if you don't join him someone else will. More significantly, God has already placed you into your timeline/reality for a reason. What is God doing where you are? How can you join with Him in that work?

Gandalf once told Frodo that "...fate rarely calls upon us in a time of our choosing." I will warn you: God's calling might not always fit your timing or even your agenda. I have had times when I planned on not going to a particular event and God said, "No, you're going." One such time was a mission trip to China. I had no job and very little money. God still sent me and provided for the trip. A significant conversation happened when I was on a train coming home. I just wanted to relax and do my devotional for the day, but the fellow next to me had left an unsupportive family, and he needed someone to talk to. I also helped him find a phone number that would be helpful.

If you look around and ask God for ideas, He will give you opportunity. Be it dangerous, exhausting, fun, or exciting you should go for such a timeline as this.

Quests of the Day:

1. Read the book of Esther.
2. Are you watching for what God is doing around you?
3. Are you in a position to influence others for Christ? If not, prayerfully brainstorm how this can change.

DAY 28: FORTIFYING AGAINST THE ZERG
BY NATHAN MARCHAND

Then I said to them, "You see the trouble we are in:
Jerusalem lies in ruins, and its gates have been burned
with fire. Come, let us rebuild the wall of Jerusalem, and
we will no longer be in disgrace." I also told them about
the gracious hand of my God on me and what the king
had said to me. They replied, "Let us start rebuilding." So
they began this good work.
Nehemiah 2:17-18

I hate the Zerg. I hate them as a race, and I hate
fighting them in the classic real-time strategy video game
StarCraft. If I say, "Zergling rush," it either drudges up feelings
of dread or sadistic glee for players.

There are three races a player can choose in *StarCraft*:
the Terrans (humans), the Zerg, and the Protoss. The Terrans
are a balanced race with heavy firepower and clever strategies.
The Protoss are a technologically-advanced, honor-bound
warrior race with powerful but expensive units that take a long
time to build but are nearly unstoppable. The Zerg are a swarm
composed of other races absorbed by biological infestation
into a hive-mind. In other words, they're an organic version of
the Borg from *Star Trek: The Next Generation*. Their trademark
gameplay is speed. They can build units quickly and cheaply,
which makes it possible for them to overwhelm opponents
before they've even built up forces.

102

In the Terran campaign mission "Desperate Alliance," the player's objective is to survive for 30 minutes. It seems simple enough, right? No. The Zerg AI is vicious. Zerglings— small beasts that function as a frontline troops—will rush the player early and often. If he manages to fight them off, they'll quickly return with larger units like Mutalisks and Hydralisks. (I assure you they're as gross as they sound).

The best strategy against this is for the player to build Marines and Firebats (Marines with flamethrowers) and embedding them in bunkers at choke points. These bunkers can be reinforced with turrets for early detection and shooting down flying Zerg. The new unit the player gets in this mission, the Vulture, is essentially a *Star Wars* speeder bike that can lay mines and fire grenades. As the mission progresses, the waves of Zerg get increasingly larger and more frequent. Bunkers will be destroyed and many of their occupants slaughtered—or eaten—by the Zerg. Build more. This requires sending vulnerable SCVs (construction units) to repair or build while protecting them with other units. If those defenses fall, so will the player.

Thankfully, though, the player just has to have one unit alive after 30 minutes to complete the mission. I know this because I completed that mission surrounded by hordes of Zerg and barely had anything other than my Command Center left.

As challenging as it is to fend off the Zerg, the titular character of the Book of Nehemiah undertook an even more challenging task: rebuilding Jerusalem. He learns that while the surviving Hebrew exiles—who'd just come out of 70 years of captivity under Babylon and Persia—had returned to Jerusalem, the city's walls and gates were in ruins. Nehemiah mourned this for many days, praying that God would forgive His people and give him favor before King Artaxerxes, whom he served as cupbearer (Nehemiah 1). The king noticed Nehemiah's grief and asked what troubled him. Nehemiah replied, "Why should my face not look sad when the city where my fathers are buried lies in ruins, and its gates have been destroyed by fire?" (Nehemiah 2:3). He goes on to tell the king that he wishes to go back to Jerusalem and rebuild it. The king simply replied, "How long will your journey take, and when will you get back?" He set a time, which the king and queen agreed to, and Nehemiah sent word to the local governors to begin making arrangements.

But he soon came against his own Zerg—in this case, three governors named Sanballat the Horonite, Tobiah the Ammonite, and Geshem the Arab (Nehemiah 2:10, 19). Nehemiah's return threatened their power in the region, so they ridiculed him and the builders. "What is this you are doing? Are you rebelling against the king?" Nehemiah, confident of the Lord's leading, retorted, "The God of heaven will give us success. We his servants will start rebuilding, but as for you, you have no share in Jerusalem or any claim or historic right to it" (Nehemiah 2:19-20). So, they continued their work in defiance. In retaliation, these governors spat slander at the Jews like Hydralisks on Terran Marines.

Many people would've succumbed to the discouragement—but not Nehemiah. He prayed,

> Hear us, O our God, for we are despised. Turn their insults back on their own heads. Give them over as plunder in a land of captivity. Do not cover up their guilt or blot out their sins from your sight, for they have thrown insults in the face of the builders (Nehemiah 4:4-5).

He and his laborers continued their work. It wasn't easy. The governors conspired against them, so Nehemiah posted armed guards at all the most vulnerable points of the walls. In fact, half of his men served as defenders while the rest did the building. Even when they went to drink water, they carried weapons with them. Restoration required vigilance. More slander followed, even threats on Nehemiah's life, but God honored their efforts, and the wall was completed. Jerusalem was safe once more, and the exiles returned to their ancestral home.

Have you longed for your own restoration? Has it been years since your life was good? Is your heart stirred by prayers pleading for more? We've all been there. I spent years at a job

I hated until God made it possible for me to start grad school and begin a new life. Like Nehemiah, though, I faced opposition. If you're about to embark on a similar path, you will, too. Don't be discouraged. If you are doing what God has called you to do, the Devil will redouble his attacks on you because now you've become a greater threat. So, take a lesson from *StarCraft*: fortify. Surround yourself with a support network—friends, family, church, etc.—who can sustain you when the Devil's "Zergling rush" comes at you. Arm yourself with the full Armor of God (Eph. 6) with Bible reading and study. Pray daily for strength. But remember that despite your vigilance, as the Petra song says, "Take courage, my friend, your redemption is near / The battle belongs to the Lord."

Quest of the Day

1. Read Nehemiah 1-2; 4; 6-7.
2. Arm yourself for daily combat by writing down a few Bible verses on some cards that you can reference throughout the day.
3. Hold a Bible study on these passages followed by a strategy board game party.

DAY 29: RAFIKI THE BAPTIST
BY ERIC ANDERSON

"…the reason I came baptizing with water was so that he
might be revealed to Israel."
John 1:31

One of my favorite Disney characters is Rafiki. He is a mentor in *The Lion King*, a baboon who acts as a priest of sorts. We first see him as he makes his way up to the top of the cliff and presents Simba, the newborn son of King Mufasa, to the crowd of thousands of animals. Before doing so he seems to put some sort of blessing on Simba. Later we find him in a tree out in isolation from the other animals. He lives a lonely and contemplative life, but he also has the respect of all the animals, except for one: Scar, Simba's uncle who betrays the royal family and uses Simba to get King Mufasa into position to be murdered.

In the New Testament we learn about another character who lived away from everyone. He lived in the wilderness, ate locusts, and often preached and baptized. His name was John the Baptist. He taught about repentance from sins and bravely called out a ruler on stealing another man's wife. Just like Rafiki, though, he had a much larger role. John was preparing the people for another man coming with a larger message. By simply pointing them to God, he was preparing the crowd for the changes Jesus would bring, just like Rafiki is part of the changes and preparations around his kingdom. One day religious leaders asked John if he was the Messiah or Elijah come back:

> John replied in the words of Isaiah the prophet: "I am the voice of one crying out in the wilderness, 'Make straight the way for the Lord….I baptize with water…but among you stands one you do not know. He is the one who comes after me, the straps of whose sandals I am not worthy to untie" (John 1:23, 27).

What John was saying was that he was charged with preparing for people for the Messiah's work by showing them their need for Him and helping them get a sense of His expectations for how to treat others.

Sometimes there is a lot of preparation for something. God might need to work on your attitude to make you ready to minister deeply to a person or group. He might want to build skills for you to use in a new position. He might just want you to learn about a culture or get to know a person before a work can begin.

One day Simba comes to Rafiki very confused and sad about missing his father. Here are a couple of Rafiki quotations:

"Change is good."

"The past can hurt, but the way I see it, you can either run from it or learn from it."

This is right when Simba moves from vagabonding with Timon and Pumbaa to fighting for his kingdom. He is hurt by the lie that he killed his father. He was so lonely and lost without his father that he needed someone to come and prepare him for the new work of taking his rightful place as king. Humanity lost their place when they allowed sin to come in, and before Jesus came to bring a new way of life to the Jews, someone was called to prepare the way for them to accept His message of love and redemption.

You might be in a place during or right before transition. There may be a lot of change coming. How is God preparing you for that?

<u>Quest of the Day</u>

1. Read Luke 3:1-18
2. How did John prepare people for Jesus coming?
3. What did he tell tax collectors and then soldiers? How is this applicable in your life?

DAY 30: NICHOLAS THE PUNISHER
BY NATHAN MARCHAND

But Zacchaeus stood up and said to the Lord, "Look, Lord!
Here and now I give half of my possessions to the poor, and
if I have cheated anybody out of anything, I will pay back
four times the amount."
Luke 19:1-10

Nicholas D. Wolfwood. This traveling priest from the sci-fi western anime/manga *Trigun* (which, interestingly, was created by a Japanese Catholic) is second only to Vash the Stampede himself as the series' most fascinating character.

When the falsely-accused outlaw Vash and his friends Meryl Stryfe and Milly Thompson (the "insurance girls") meet Wolfwood, he's sitting in the middle of the desert, seemingly dead, but revives quickly when the bus passengers investigate him. He wears sunglasses and carries a massive cross wrapped in cloth and belts. When someone asks if this cross is heavy, Wolfwood replies with one of the best (and most profound) lines of the show: "That's because it's so full of mercy." He's as goofy as Vash, making Meryl remark that they're perfect for each other. However, he sees through Vash's façade, saying the outlaw's demeanor hides a far more tragic internal struggle. They then save the passengers from robots, Wolfwood revealing that his cross is the Punisher, a massive machine gun and armory harboring multiple handguns in the crossbeam.

Vash is astonished at the priest's accuracy, which is the audience's first clue that Wolfwood is hiding a dark side.

After a few more adventures, Wolfwood says Knives, Vash's evil brother, may have caused the inhabitants of the town Carcases to disappear. When the group arrives there, we have the "Shyamalan twist"—Wolfwood was hired by Knives to keep his brother alive until their final confrontation. Now, though, Wolfwood's mentor/handler, Chapel the Evergreen, tells him that his orders have changed: he is to kill Vash. If not, the orphanage Wolfwood has been supporting with the money he earned as an assassin will be massacred. Wolfwood leaves to contemplate his decisions. Vash started as a job, but now he had become a friend whose pacifistic ideals of helping others without killing villains had left an undeniable impression on him.

The next day, he confronts Chapel, defeating him and sparing his life. But Knives' minion, the telekinetic Legato Bluesummers, takes control of Chapel's arm to shoot Wolfwood. A gunshot echoes through the town. He meets Vash to comfort him after failing to prevent someone from committing suicide and tells him where his brother is located. Vash says he never told Wolfwood about his brother, but the priest has vanished.

Then in one of the greatest death scenes in all of anime, Wolfwood, walks into a church carrying Punisher, bleeding, and collapses in front of the altar. He prays,

> I did what it took to protect the children at any cost. That's how I always justified my actions. I took many people's lives, believing there was no other way. My sins are so heavy…too heavy…too heavy to ever atone for. And yet, somehow, I feel happy, at peace with myself today. It really can be done. Once you stop to think about it, there are plenty of ways to save everyone. Why didn't I ever listen to him? Why didn't I see that before it was too late?

He goes on to say,

> Was everything in my life a mistake? Would I be wrong now to ask for your forgiveness? *I did not want to die this way!*

His hand falls to the floor, and his eyes slowly close, a smile on his face, as he leans against his cross-shaped weapon.

While a bit less dramatic, Luke 19:1-10 tells the story of a sinner who was changed by an encounter with Jesus: Zacchaeus the tax collector. He was the top dog in the region. In Jewish culture, though, tax collectors were reviled. They were seen as traitorous frauds who collected more money than they needed to line their own pockets while serving Israel's Roman overlords. Throughout the Gospels the Pharisees try to slander Jesus by saying he "eats with tax collectors and 'sinners.'" This profession is singled out from "sinners" as exceptionally evil. So, Zacchaeus is wealthy but hated.

However, he was desperate to see Jesus. Unfortunately, he was as short as Vizzini from *The Princess Bride*, so he climbed a sycamore tree to get above the thick crowd. Not only was he able to see Jesus, but Jesus saw him. (Given that sycamore trees were 30-40 feet tall, Zacchaeus would've been easy to spot—because he's a spider monkey). Then in a move that illustrates Jesus' teaching on the shepherd who leaves the 99 sheep to seek the one that was lost (Matt. 18:12; Luke 15:4), He looked up at the tax collector and said, "Zacchaeus, come down immediately. I must stay at your house today" (Luke 19:5). He wasted no time climbing down and welcoming Jesus into his home.

As usual, the people saw this as scandalous. Verse seven says, "All the people saw this and began to mutter, 'He has gone to be the guest of a sinner.'" Perhaps they were jealous that Jesus chose this reviled tax collector to stay with instead of one of them. Whatever the reason, Zacchaeus took it in stride, saying, "Look, Lord! Here and now I give half of my possessions to the poor, and if I have cheated anybody out of anything, I will pay back four times the amount" (Luke 19:8). This wasn't an arbitrary number; it was the required repayment for theft in the Mosaic Law (Ex. 22:1). But he didn't stop there. Half of everything he owned would be given away. His goal was to get right with God and others *and* do right by those less unfortunate than himself. All because he met Jesus.

So impressed was Christ with Zacchaeus, he said, "Today salvation has come to this house, because this man, too, is a son of Abraham. For the Son of Man came to seek and to save the lost" (Luke 19:9-10).

Have you experienced this renewed life in Christ? It's one thing to convert to Christianity and repent of your sins. It's another thing entirely to experience the *zoe* (Greek for "spiritual life") that comes from repentance. Wolfwood thought he was doing the right thing by working as an assassin-for-hire to raise money for orphans. Zacchaeus undoubtedly grew up hearing about the Law and the prophets. But they both strayed from the righteous path until they met a man who made them rethink their lives and change their ways. Not by preaching at them, but by simply being themselves.

Jesus has more to give you than just salvation. As He said in John 10:10b, "I have come that they may have life, and have it to the full." He wants to give you the life you were meant to live before sin marred it; one of love and joy and the rest of the fruit of spirit (Gal. 5:22). Jesus isn't content to stop at your repentance. That's only the first step. He wants to give you new life that it might overflow into all those around you.

Because He's so full of mercy.

Quest of the Day

1. Read Luke 19:1-10.

2. Have you wronged someone recently (or not-so-recently)? Go to the Lord in prayer to repent of that sin. Journal about it.

3. What can you do to atone for the sin you committed against that person? Repay them money? Send a card with an apology? Ask for forgiveness? Write down a few ideas and enact them this week.

DAY 31: THE R.A.C., ANT-MAN AND CONVICTION
BY ERIC ANDERSON

"Has no one condemned you? Neither do I."
John 8:10-11

Have you ever been caught in your own failure? Everyone around you knows you messed up. They are angry with you, doubting you, and condemning you. Maybe you even pay for it or apologize or somehow make amends. Still, they hound you or ignore you or refuse to leave you alone. Jesus met many people in these circumstances.

In John 8 a woman was caught in adultery. Some religious leaders brought her to Jesus as a test. They wanted to test Jesus and figured they'd deal with a "sinner" with one "stone," as the phrase goes. Jesus had a lot of choices. He could have thrown a stone or he could have told them to do so. He could have berated the woman or berated the men for not bringing her adulterous lover. Instead, he wrote in the sand. Then he looked at the men, who all had stones to throw at her, and said one simple thing: "Whoever is without sin may throw the first stone." Shocked, the men slowly, beginning with the eldest, dropped their stones and walked away. He turned to the woman, "Does anyone now stand condemning you? Neither do I. Go and sin no more."

In a flashback episode of the TV show *Killjoys* titled "The Warrior Princess Bride," Dutch and Johnny are duped when someone has them take some materials to the quad that were not exactly legal. Having never been to the quad, they are unprepared. An assassin used them to get into town, and the R.A.C. (Recovery and Apprehension Coalition—basically galactic bounty hunters) needs to catch this assassin. Instead of throwing them in jail or kicking them out, the R.A.C. sends them on a mission to find and catch the assassin. After this is successful, Dutch and Johnny are offered a job with the R.A.C. They are already doing dangerous work to get by, so this is right up their alley.

Consider Ant-Man in his movie. Scott Lang has a rap sheet. He had stolen from a large company and paid his dues in prison, but he still could not get or keep a job, especially after lying about it to an ice cream company that always finds out. So, he breaks into a house to get a score. He doesn't find much aside from some weird suit, and he is arrested rather quickly. But then the owner of the house comes to him with an offer he cannot refuse. He still needs to do something illegal, but at least someone has seen something in him. Someone gives him an opportunity when no one else would.

Condemnation is not the only issue that causes us to feel like an outcast, but it is a major one. When you feel outcast and someone recognizes you or does one kind act for you, it can bring healing, hope, and relief. With the adulterous woman, Jesus actually stopped the condemnation. Some theorize that his writing in the sand may have been the sins of the men planning to stone her. But He did not agree with her act, either. He told her, "Go and sin no more." He still cared enough to give her hope and point her in a new direction.

Do you know the difference between condemnation and conviction? Condemnation limits eyesight to the sin. It sees nothing more than your poor choices and rebellion against God. Conviction sees what you can become. It sees your possible future in Christ and beckons you forward as a new creation. Condemnation says, "You are the sin," while conviction says, "You have sinned, but you can do better." Jesus convicts us of our sin, and with that conviction He calls us into a future filled with hope and a relationship with Him.

Quests of the Day

1. Read John 8:1-11
2. Is there someone who is an outcast that you can help?
3. If you are following Jesus, share a way he has helped you change with someone. If you are not, see if you can find someone who can share their story with you.

DAY 32: EVERY WORD OF WHAT YOU JUST SAID WAS WRONG
BY NATHAN MARCHAND

"I am not possessed by a demon," said Jesus, "but I honor
my Father and you dishonor me."
John 8:49

I love *Star Wars: The Last Jedi* in large part because it is
one of the most thematically rich films in the franchise. (Odds
say half of you just quit reading. For those who stayed, thank
you). Much ado has been made about old Luke Skywalker, but
truthfully he's a huge part of why I love the film.

The ragtag Resistance is pinned down in a fortified
stronghold on the planet Crait with the overwhelming forces
of the First Order, under the command of the newly self-
appointed Supreme Leader Kylo Ren, about to blast their way
into the rebel base with a massive siege cannon. All hope is
lost.

Until the legendary Luke Skywalker arrives.

Earlier in the film while teaching the young heroine
Rey the ways of the Force, he told her, "You think what? I'm
gonna walk out with a laser sword and face down the whole
First Order?" The Jedi Master had become a cynical hermit.
He failed to prevent his nephew, Ben Solo (aka Kylo Ren),
from turning to the Dark Side, and for a fleeting moment
considered murdering him. This led to the destruction of

Luke's Jedi academy by his nephew. Now the call to action had come to him again with the pleading words of Rey, but only after some wise counsel from the Force ghost of Yoda does Luke heed this call and, ironically, do exactly what he sarcastically said he would.

So, after a brief meeting with his twin sister, General Leia, and surviving a barrage of laser cannon fire from AT-ATs (with a truly anime-esque shoulder wipe), Kylo Ren goes down to confront him.

"Did you come back here to say you forgive me? To save my soul?"

"No," Luke replies.

They draw lightsabers, and Kylo lashes out in rage, but Luke parries and blocks everything effortlessly. He makes Kylo look like a chump.

"I failed you, Ben. I'm sorry."

"I'm sure you are! The Resistance is dead! The war is over! And when I kill you, I will have killed the last Jedi!"

Luke retorts with something similar that he'd said to Rey during their lessons: "Amazing! Every word of what you just said was wrong. The Rebellion is reborn today. The war is just beginning. And I will not be the last Jedi."

"I'll destroy you…and her…and all of it!"

Luke extinguishes his lightsaber. "No. Strike me down in anger, and I'll always be with you. Just like your father."

Kylo lashes out and finally gets a hit—only to learn that the Luke he is fighting is an astral projection.

"See you around, kid," Luke says, and vanishes.

The Gospels are full of passages where Jesus is questioned by many people: His disciples, the Jews, the Gentiles. Many were curious to hear what He had to say. The Pharisees and the Sadducees, though, were Jesus' most infamous enemies. They were elitist religious sects within Jewish culture. They used their positions to oppress others because they thought they were smarter and holier.

John 8 includes a particularly potent exchange between Jesus and the Pharisees. After soundly defeating the Pharisees in their attempt to trap him with the woman caught in adultery, the rest of the chapter is a verbal barrage between Jesus, the Pharisees, and unbelieving Jews. Here are a few examples:

Pharisees: "Here you are, appearing as your own witness; your testimony is not valid."
Jesus: "Even if I testify on my own behalf, my testimony is valid, for I know where I come from and where I am going. But you have no idea where I come from or where I am going" (v. 13-14).

Jesus: "I am going away, and you will look for me, and you will die in your sin. Where I go, you cannot come."

Jews: "Will he kill himself? Is that why he says, 'Where I go, you cannot come'?"

Jesus: "You are from below; I am from above. You are of this world; I am not of this world. I told you would die in your sins; if you do not believe that I am the one I claim to be, you will indeed die in your sins" (v. 21-24).

Jews: Aren't we right in saying that you are a Samaritan and   demon-possessed?"

Jesus: "I am not possessed by a demon, but I honor my Father and you dishonor me. I am not seeking glory for myself; but there is one who seeks it, and he is the judge" (v. 48-50).

By the end of it, Jesus declared Himself "I AM," an emphatic statement that made Him equal with God. Incensed, the crowds picked up rocks to stone Jesus as a blasphemer, but He "hid himself, slipping away from the temple grounds" (v. 59).

Jesus was what author John Eldredge called a "beautiful outlaw." He challenged the status quo. He questioned the Pharisees' interpretations of Scripture. He came to free the people from their sins since the law had done nothing but burden them with condemnation. The religious leaders took advantage of this system for their own gains. But when confronted with laser-like questions, Jesus shrugged them off like Luke Skywalker the not-quite-last-Jedi.

It takes courage to stand for the Truth (capital T). Like Jesus, you'll be questioned about why you believe what you believe. Like Luke, you must be ready to stand firm. Your enemy, the Devil, will do everything he can to stop you. It's then that something said by Dr. Wes Gerig, one of me and Eric's Bible professors, must become your mantra: "Never forget in the darkness what God has shown you in the light."

If you need a one-liner when that time comes, perhaps try, "See you around, Devil."

Quest of the Day

1. Read John 8.
2. What is a question the Devil plagues you with? Write it down. Identify the lie.
3. Once you do that, write a short prayer that you can use to answer the question and counteract the lie.

Day 33: Lamb of Crucifixion, Lion of Resurrection
By: Eric Anderson

"The Son of Man must suffer many things and be rejected by
the elders and chief priests and scribes, and be killed and be
raised up on the third day."
Luke 9:22

We were fighting a tough battle in Sentinels of the
Multiverse, a cooperative card game that allows the players to
be superheroes and unite to fight a supervillain. Each hero has
their own deck that each player can us. The villain has his/her
own deck which works with its own turn. Also included is an
environment, which again has its own deck. There are many
environments, including a land with dinosaurs, the city of
Megalopolis, and even a realm where time and space are
distorted called the Final Wasteland. I was playing as the
Naturalist, a character that can turn into three different animals
similar to Beast Boy from DC Comics. As the game went on,
the villain kept caging me, but while I kept his attention with
that cage, my teammates were bringing down his health.
Finally, I broke out of the cage in crocodile form and snapped
down on the villain, gaining the victory for our team.

Jesus also has been described in terms of animals, but
He doesn't shapeshift into them. In one place we see him
described as a lion. Lions are powerful. They need strong cages
at the zoo and are thought of as scary animals in the wild. They

are animals of power, often seen as the top of the food chain. We also see Jesus described as a lamb. Lambs are simple, peaceful, and have no power. We don't need strong cages for them, and although all animals can be dangerous, these tend to be calm and easygoing.

Jesus is known for a particular dilemma. He had been arrested and was on trial in front of Governor Pontius Pilate. Would he prove to be the lion by responding with power that would terrify the governor and end the long line of accusations? Or would he be the lamb by sitting there, taking the heat, and allowing his accusers to walk all over Him? He even admitted to Peter at his arrest that he could call down a host of angels to his defense. But that was not the plan. The plan was to be a lamb. Lambs were used in Israel for sacrifices for hundreds of , and this was no different. Jesus had not sinned, and there was no reason to condemn him, but the religious leaders insisted and God chose to use this evil.

This was for the ultimate terraforming. Man had been stuck in sin for centuries, and the time had finally come to build a bridge of salvation. Jesus was that bridge. The sinless man, the second Adam (see 1 Corinthians 15:45), took our sin upon Himself and chose to be our atonement, our sacrificial lamb.

> For while we were still helpless, at the right time Christ died
> for the ungodly. For one will hardly die for a righteous man;
> though perhaps for the good man someone would dare even

to die. But God demonstrates His own love toward us, in that while we were yet sinners, Christ died for us. Much more then, having now been justified by His blood, we shall be saved from the wrath of God through Him" (Romans 5:6-9, NASB).

Imagine that. The ultimate act of terraforming came not through power or militarism, but through the selfless, meek non-action of a Lamb. Even while being accused, Jesus did not speak and stood there with no response. He did not fight by arguing or by striking the religious leaders and army down. He won by losing.

But three days later, Jesus chose the Lion card. The earth rumbled, the stone was rolled away, and Jesus came out of the grave! Indeed, his loss came with great reward as Jesus became the first resurrection. His power came throughout his time in ministry by teaching truth to those who didn't want to hear it. Now, his power proved full as He resurrected from the dead, defeating death itself. Jesus had defeated sickness, delivered people from demonic oppression, and had raised a man from the dead, yet this resurrection of His was a new declaration of grace and hope for all who are willing to trust in Him.

Quest of the Day

1. Read Romans 5.

2. Recommended reading: If you have questions about the validity of the resurrection or other big questions, try *The Case for Christ* by Lee Strobel.

DAY 34: HEART OF THE SWORD
BY NATHAN MARCHAND

Jesus replied, "Blessed are you, Simon son of Jonah, for this
was not revealed to you by flesh and blood, but by my Father
in heaven. And I tell you that you are Peter, and on this rock
I will build my church, and the gates of Hades will not
overcome it."
Matthew 16:17-18

Seijûrô Hiko XIII, a powerful master swordsman of
the Hiten-Mitsurugi style, wanders the countryside until he
comes upon bandits massacring a caravan late one night in the
beginning the anime OVA (original video animation) *Samurai
X: Trust and Betrayal* (an adaptation of a flashback storyline
from the manga *Rurouni Kenshin*). He kills the bandits but finds
there is only one survivor: a small red-haired boy. "You may
hate these murderers," he tells him as he cleans his sword, "but
that will not bring your family back. Let your survival be your
family's memorial." In the manga, he tells the boy to go to the
nearby town for help. Hearing no word of a child visiting that
town, Master Hiko assumes he committed suicide and returns
to the site of the bloodbath to bury the dead. But to his
surprise, he finds a makeshift graveyard with wooden crosses
and a few stones for markers. At the center stands the boy he
had saved.

"You dug graves for your family and their murderers."

"This wasn't my family," replies the boy. "They were slave traders. I was sold to them after my parents died. Last night they stopped being traders or murderers. They were all just victims."

Master Hiko notices three stones in front of the boy and asks him about them. The child says those are the grave markers for three young women who died protecting him from the bandits. He wanted their graves to be beautiful, but all he could find were ugly rocks. "I wish I had flowers," he laments. "They all deserve flowers." Master Hiko uncorks his sake bottle and pours it on the stones, saying, "No one should reach Nirvana without the taste of good sake on his lips. This is my tribute to them." He then introduces himself as the boy's new master.

"Listen," he says to him, "you were unable to save the lives of the women who took care of you. Now your inner self is laden with their memories. Your small hands can attest to the weight of their lifeless bodies. However, you will learn that their memories are heavier, and carrying them will make your stronger. This new strength will be your defense and aid in the protection of that which is truly important. But this can only happen if you are properly trained. What is your name?"

"Shinta," he replies.

"A child's name. Too soft for a swordsman. As of today, you are Kenshin." This is a name that in Japanese means "heart of the sword."

The Bible records several instances where God changes someone's name. Eric wrote about Abram becoming Abraham on day nine, but there's also Jacob becoming Israel (Genesis 32:28) and, to a lesser extent, Saul becoming Paul (you'll read about that on day 36). Not only was this God's way of giving them a new identity, but each one of these happened at a key moment in biblical history. Today's foreshadowed what might be the second most important event in world history (next to the death and resurrection of Christ).

John 1 records that when John the Baptist and two of his disciples saw Jesus walk by, the Baptist again declared Him "the Lamb of God." The two disciples, one of whom was future Apostle Andrew, followed Jesus, spending the entire day with Him. Andrew then did what any of us nerds/geeks do when we discover a cool new thing: he rushed home and told his brother, Simon. "We have found the Messiah," he told him (John 1:41b). Andrew took Simon to meet Jesus, which led to one of those world-altering moments. "'You are Simon son of John. You will be called Cephas' (which, when translated, is Peter)" (John 1:42b).

However, the significance of this name isn't revealed until later. In Matthew 16:13, Jesus asked His disciples, "Who do people say the Son of Man is?" After they shared a few answers—including the great prophet Elijah, among others— He asks, "Who do you say I am?" Peter answers, "You are the Christ, the Son of the living God" (Matt. 16:16). In response, Jesus says,

> "Blessed are you, Simon son of Jonah, for this was not revealed to you by flesh and blood, but by my Father in heaven. And I tell you that you are Peter, and on this rock I will build my church, and the gates of Hades will not overcome it. I will give you the keys of the kingdom of heaven; whatever you bind on earth will be bound in heaven, and whatever you loose on earth will be loosed in heaven" (Matt. 16:17-18).

In Greek the name Peter is *Petra*, which means, "rock." When the Day of Pentecost came (see Eric's entry on day 35), Peter became the first leader of the early church. In Catholic tradition, he is the first pope. In other words, God used him to establish the Christian church, which then spread across the world for centuries. Is it any wonder why Jesus changed his name? Such an undertaking would require a radical transformation of identity, especially in the ancient world when a person's name carried great importance.

God offers this same identity to you. Each of us has a purpose to which He has called us, but in order to live this new destiny, we must shed our old lives. This requires a renewing of our very selves. Have you been labeled by others? Do their insults—the "names" they gave you—still haunt you? Jesus wishes to give you a new name befitting His new purposes for you. In fact, Revelation 2:17 says Jesus will give "to those who overcome...a white stone with a new name written on it, known only to him who receives it." While it's a strange verse in a strange book of the Bible, it speaks to this new identity. You are defined by God and not the world.

So, whether you be a rock or the heart of the sword, take hold of this new name and forge ahead.

Quest of the Day

1. Read John 1:19-42 and Matthew 16:13-20.

2. What are the "names" you've been labeled by others? These could be insults from bullies or enemies ("Fat," "Ugly," "Idiot," etc.) or the expectations put on you by your parents. Whatever they are, write them down. When you're finished, take that paper and either rip it up or burn it as a symbolic gesture of shedding those old names.

3. Spend some time in prayer asking God to reveal to you your new name. Let this be a step toward understanding your new identity in Christ.

Day 35: Computers, Pentecost, and "Synths"
By Eric Anderson

All of them were filled with the Holy Spirit....
Acts 2:4

Long ago, computers were huge! They took up whole rooms, and you could only find a few here and there. They were only available for companies and maybe a few scientists. Now everyone has a computer. Why? In the 1970s an engineer named Ted Hoff invented a micro-processor that could do the same work as ENIAC (a large, room-sized computer used for complex math such as missile trajectories). Then a company called MITS created build-a-kits for computers using these processors. You could order it and build it yourself after it was delivered. Then Microsoft created what they called "personal computers," and a year later Steve Jobs and Steve Wozniak built a company called Apple that eventually created iPods. Computers were everywhere. It took years of development and a huge shift in culture, but they are now carried in our pockets.

There was a day in history called Pentecost. Pentecost comes from the Greek for "fiftieth," and this event happened 50 days after the crucifixion, which was on Passover. This was another Jewish festival called the Feast of Weeks: a celebratory festival thanking God for the spring harvest. On this day, the disciples were in a room together early in the morning. Acts 2 tells us they saw what looked like tongues of fire coming down, splitting apart and resting on each of their heads. It sounded like a violent wind was blowing through their room, and immediately they were different. They walked out and began speaking languages they didn't know. Before this, the Holy Spirit had been felt and revealed in a few individuals called prophets. Now, He was available to fill any human who accepted Jesus as "the Way, the Truth, and the Life" (John 14:6). What took humans years in technology took God a few moments to do for our souls.

The response was a lot of confusion. How could all these uneducated men from a backwater region of Israel know all these languages? Some thought they were drunk and others laughed at the whole thing. Peter stood up and spoke. He quoted the prophet Joel and David and reminded them of Jesus' work. When asked what they should do, Peter said:

> "Repent and be baptized, every one of you, in the name of Jesus Christ for the forgiveness of your sins. *And you will receive the gift of the Holy Spirit.* The promise is for you and your children and for all who are far off—for all whom the Lord our God will call: (Acts 2:38-39, emphasis added).

At the end of season two of *Humans*, everything changed. *Humans* is a look at what might happen if we had androids that were closely identical to us. It asks the question, "What makes us human?" It follows a small group of "Synths" who are self-aware as well as a few humans who interact with them. Lucy managed to get a new source code out, which had been created by the original designer of the "Synths," and in season three we see the fallout, both good and bad, of this decision. A few Synths begin to show consciousness, but this changes it all. Now, thousands of them are waking up. They start to realize they are slaves, gain emotions, take an interest in hobbies, and become more self-aware.

Pentecost was a download for the human condition; a download of the Holy Spirit for all humans who would follow Jesus. In both of these cases, there was a new form of self from an outside source. "Synths" were able to experience life and understood the experience of feeling loss, victory, loneliness, and even a desire for rights. For the disciples, this meant a new experience of God Himself. Not becoming God, but a new way to experience Him regularly and to share Him and His hope, purpose, and grace with everyone they met. This was not meant to be a one-time deal. Today we are given the opportunity to regularly experience Jesus through the Holy Spirit. He wants to guide us, give us hope, give us spiritual gifts (i.e. superpowers to use for His glory) and walk with us in painful situations.

Have you explored all of the downloads Jesus offers you in the Holy Spirit?

Quest of the Day:

135

1. Read Acts 2.

2. Ask the Holy Spirit to guide you through the next 24 hours. He might guide through small whispers or through unexpected interactions with others.

DAY 36: GODZILLA AND THE DAMASCUS ROAD
BY NATHAN MARCHAND

But the Lord said to Ananias, "Go! This man is my
chosen instrument to carry my name before the Gentiles
and their kings and the people of Israel."
Acts 9:15

In 1964's *Ghidorah, the Three-Headed Monster*, the fifth
entry of the Showa (or classic) Godzilla series by Toho, a
princess disappears in an exploding plane. She reappears later
as a Venusian (Martian in the dubbed version) prophetess
foretelling the coming of giant monsters. Her prophecies keep
coming true. Rodan rises from a volcano. Godzilla emerges
from the ocean. But the most terrifying of all is King Ghidorah,
a three-headed golden space dragon (and yes, he's as awesome
as that sounds) who emerges from a crashed meteorite. This
Lovecraftian beast destroyed the prophetess' civilization
millennia ago, and now intends to devastate Earth.

Godzilla and Rodan, though, are more interested in
fighting each other near Mt. Fuji. The larva of the insect
goddess Mothra is led to the mountain by her tiny twin
priestesses, the Shobijin, where she goes full-tilt mom on the
overgrown dinosaurs. She covers them with silk webbing to
make them stop and listen to her, but despite her reminding
the kaiju (giant monsters) that Earth is where they keep their
stuff, they refuse to fight Ghidorah because humanity always

attacks them. Desperate, Mothra decides to battle the space monster herself, much to the shock of Godzilla and Rodan.

Predictably, Ghidorah's lightning-like gravity beams toss Mothra around like a toy. All hope seems lost.

Until Godzilla makes a heroic charge.

Rodan, too, quickly swoops in.

By their powers combined (No-Prize to everyone who got that reference), the three-headed monster is defeated and sent running back into outer space.

This was a turning point for Godzilla. After menacing Japan as an atomic force of nature for a decade, he became its new hero. For the rest of the Showa series, he would defend Japan from all manner of kaiju, robots, and alien invaders. Monsters that were once his enemies, like Rodan and Anguirus, became his staunchest allies. By the 1970s, he was practically a superhero.

One of the most dramatic conversion stories in the Bible is found in Acts, and like Godzilla, it came about from an encounter with divinity. Saul of Tarsus was a Pharisee of Pharisees (Phil. 3:5). As the Church grew by leaps and bounds, the Pharisees saw it as a threat to their power. So, they persecuted it. In fact, Acts 7:54-60 records the death of Stephen, the first Christian martyr, after an exhaustive speech before the Sanhedrin recounting the history of Israel that ended with him indicting the religious leaders. They dragged him out of the city and stoned him to death, though he prayed, "Lord Jesus, receive my spirit," and, "Lord, do not hold this sin against them" (Acts 7:59-60). The story ends with the first verse of Acts 8: "And Saul approved of their killing him." There's no mention of him participating, but he certainly condoned it.

He continued to "breath[e] out murderous threats against the Lord's disciples" (Acts 9:1). On his journey to Damascus in search of Christ-followers to imprison, Saul had a close encounter:

> As he neared Damascus on his journey, suddenly a light from heaven flashed around him. He fell to the ground and heard a voice say to him, "Saul, Saul, why do you persecute me?"
>
> "Who are you, Lord?" Saul asked.
>
> "I am Jesus, whom you are persecuting," he replied. "Now get up and go into the city, and you will be told what you must do."
>
> (Acts 9:3-6)

He was struck blind—as one would expect seeing the face of God—and had to be led into the city. For three days he ate and drank nothing.

The Lord commanded Ananias to go to the house where Saul was staying. Ananias replied, "I have heard many reports about this man and all the harm he has done to your holy people in Jerusalem. And he has come here with authority from the chief priests to arrest all who call on your name" (Acts 9:13-14). But the Lord makes Himself quite clear, saying, "Go! This man is my chosen instrument to proclaim my name to the Gentiles and their kings and to the people of Israel. I will show him how much he must suffer for my name" (v. 15-16).

Ananias went to Saul, placed his hands on Saul's eyes, and said, "Brother Saul, the Lord—Jesus, who appeared to you on the road as you were coming here—has sent me so that you may see again and be filled with the Holy Spirit" (v. 17). Then literal scales (suddenly the Godzilla analogy doesn't seem that weird, does it?) fell from Saul's eyes, and he could see again. Immediately, he was baptized and fed. In no time he was in the local synagogues preaching about Jesus Christ. To say the people were baffled would be an understatement: "Isn't he the man who raised havoc in Jerusalem among those who call on this name? And hasn't he come here to take them as prisoners to the chief priests?" (v. 21). Even so, Saul would go on to become the Apostle Paul, one of the early Church's most powerful evangelists and the author of two-thirds of the New Testament.

Many of you lived lives not unlike that of Saul/Paul and Godzilla. Perhaps you were once an atheist who opposed Christians at every turn. Maybe you were member of another religion. You may have committed horrible sins. I once had a pastor who told me that if it wasn't for Jesus, he'd either be dead or in jail.

That's why stories like this are inspiring. God, in one of the great ironies of history, took one of the Church's greatest enemies and made him one of its greatest champions. He used Paul's connections, Roman citizenship, and knowledge to preach the Gospel in places no one else could. Paul made several missionary journeys across the Roman Empire, planting churches wherever he went. It's because of him that Gentiles like me and (most of) you reading this know who Christ is.

The same God who turned a persecutor into a preacher can do the same for you! No matter your past, God can redeem it for His glory and make you a powerful instrument in His service.

To which I say to you, "Go, go, Godzilla!"

<u>Quest of the Day</u>

1. Read Acts 9.

2. Make a list of subcultures you were or are involved with that are in desperate need of Jesus Christ.

3. Once you have that list, do an internet search to see if there are ministries dedicated to reaching out to those subcultures. For example, if you're a video gamer, look up Love Thy Nerd.

DAY 37: PETER AND THE CORNY JOCK
BY ERIC ANDERSON

"And through your offspring all nations on Earth will be
blessed."
Genesis 22:18

In a season four episode of *The Big Bang Theory* titled
"The Justice League Recombination," it's almost New Year's
Eve, and the guys are planning their celebration, which will
involve time at the comic store party. The party includes a
costume contest with a prize for best group cosplay. Leonard
asks Penny to join them for the night's festivities dressed as
Wonder Woman. To his angst, she is back with her old
boyfriend: a jock of all jocks named Zack. This guy is missing
a few fries from his Happy Meal and is very interested in
sports, with the muscles and height to go along with it.

Walowitz comes up with an idea. "Why don't we have
him come along? Look at him. He can be Superman!"

There are mixed feelings. Leonard and the guys are not
happy about including the jock. But Zack loves the idea of
going to the comic store for New Year's Eve, and he especially
likes the opportunity to be Superman for the group in the
cosplay contest. Penny isn't so sure, but Walowitz wins. Penny
cosplays as Wonder Woman, Zack as Superman, and Leonard
as Green Lantern. The other guys do Batman, the Flash and

Aquaman. They have a pretty decent night, even winning the contest.

I know some nerds and geeks who love *The Big Bang Theory* and some who hate it, but if you look at this story, you see a poignant opportunity for truth: people are not meant to be jerks to each other because of their differences. Spoiler Alert: God loves everyone, and that includes the jerk of a jock next door and the woman down the street who irritates you. He also loves the high-minded nerds (like some guy who gets a spin-off about his childhood) who think they know everything.

From the get-go God's plan for salvation and His plan for newness was not meant just for the Jews or any one race to control. He told Abraham that the whole world would be blessed through His line (Gen. 22:18). In the lineage of Jesus we find a Gentile prostitute as well as King David. In the law we find requirements to welcome the foreigner and alien into the fold and to take care of their needs.

Acts 10-11 records that Peter had to face these issues. He was sitting on the roof waiting for a meal when he fell into a trance. During this he saw a vision of a sheet being lowered from Heaven with various unclean animals; animals a Jew was not supposed to eat. He refused, but God said, "Do not call anything impure that God has made clean" (Acts 10:15). This was repeated before the sheet was raised. As Peter was coming out of the trance, men came from a Roman Centurion named Cornelius. Centurions were not exactly seen as a Jew's best friend and were supposedly the worst of the Gentiles. Yet this particular commander was God-fearing and charitable. Peter was asked to come to Caesarea to share his message, and so he did with Cornelius, who had gathered his whole family, and his close friends. As he was speaking, the Holy Spirit descended upon the room, and all these Gentiles started speaking in tongues. Peter was amazed and then ordered that they be baptized with water.

When the news of Gentiles speaking in tongues and following Jesus reached the ears of the brothers in Jerusalem, they were not happy. Peter was pulled into a long meeting to talk about this. He shared his story with them, and the six men who had travelled with him to meet Cornelius also came and shared what they had seen and heard. After hearing such testimony they started praising God. Salvation was now available for all who would believe.

Is there a person you would never believe could follow Jesus? Is there a person with a different hobby you have a hard time working alongside or someone who has ridiculed the hobbies you love? Even for them Jesus came to die and resurrect. Paul tells us that, "There is neither Jew nor Gentile, neither slave nor free, nor is there male and female, for you are all one in Christ Jesus" (Galatians 3:28). We could add, "Nerd or Jock."

How can you be a friend in Christ to them?

<u>Quest of the Day:</u>

1. Read Acts 10-11:1-18.

2. Brainstorm simple actions you can do to show love to someone different from you.

3. Do some of these actions.

DAY 38: OPTIMAL OPTIMUS
BY NATHAN MARCHAND

Therefore if anyone is in Christ, he is a new creation. The
old has gone, the new has come!
2 Corinthians 5:17

"Say goodbye to the universe, Maximals! The future
has   changed, yessssss.   The   Autobots lose!
Evil triumphs! And you…you no longer exist!"

Like any great supervaillain, Megatron in the CGI *Beast
Wars* cartoon never could resist the urge to gloat.

All joking aside, this was the direst crisis the heroic
Maximals (descendants of the Autobots) had faced in their
guerilla war against the evil Predacons (descendants of the
Decepticons). At end of the show's second season, they learn
the planet they crashed on was actually ancient Earth. Not only
that, but Megatron discovers the location of the Ark, the ship
that transported a group of Autobots and Decepticons to
Earth four million years before 1984. He boards the ship, finds
the unconscious body of Optimus Prime—and gives him the
mother of all headshots. With Prime dead, a time storm erupts
as reality unravels.

It was a long summer waiting out that cliffhanger.

In the next episode, "Optimal Situation," the Maximals
and the Predacon turncoat Blackarachnia are able to stabilize

Prime and the time storm, but the Autobot leader's spark—his soul—is still fading. Since a spark can't exist outside a living body, Maximal commander Optimus Primal volunteers to house Prime's spark inside himself. It's an excruciating process. Prime's spark is powerful, and Primal screams in agony. Primal's body—for lack of a better term—mutates. A few minutes later, he stands a reborn robot: taller, more colorful, more metallic, and now possessing four modes (robot, ape, jet, and armored transport). He inherited some of the Autobot leader's traits. Primal even talks like Prime throughout the episode. At one point he tells off Megatron by saying Prime's well-known mantra, "Freedom is the right of all sentient beings," and he commands his fellow Maximals to "Transform and *roll out!*"

As Primal takes flight in his jet mode, the young Cheetor remarks, "Jumping gyros, Optimus sure learns a new body fast!" To which the snarky Rattrap quips, "Well, wha'd ya expect? He changes 'em often enough!" (cue rimshot).

By the end of the episode, Prime's body is repaired and Primal returns the spark to its rightful place. The Autobot awakens briefly, making eye contact with Primal, who sees a swirling galaxy in Prime's eyes until he once again falls asleep.

In 2 Corinthians 5, the Apostle Paul speaks a great deal about "new bodies": "For we know that if the earthly tent we live in is destroyed, we have a building from God, an eternal house in heaven, not built by human hands" (v. 1). He's speaking of the uncorrupted, redeemed bodies Christians will receive in Heaven. In our earthly lives, we "groan" (v. 2) as we wait in expectant hope for God to keep this glorious promise.

The amazing thing is He has given Christians the Holy Spirit as a "deposit" (v. 5) for what is to come. By indwelling the believer, He begins to transform him into a holier version of himself. In other words, the Spirit helps the Christian become the person God created him to be. By extension He imparts Christ's resurrection power in his life, giving the believer the ability to overcome the obstacles before him. This is a foretaste of eternity. This is why Paul famously said in verse eight, "We live by faith and not by sight." We haven't seen the full glory of what is to come, but the Spirit reminds us of it daily.

We are no longer the "totally depraved" people we were before coming to Christ (though we still struggle with sin). We are a "new creation; the old has gone, the new has come!" (v. 17). Because of this, we are reconciled to God and work as His ambassadors in the ministry of reconciliation (v. 18-20). The transformative power we have experienced is to be shared with others, for God doesn't desire that any should perish (2 Peter 3:9).

Optimus Primal experienced a similar transformation when he housed the spark of Optimus Prime. Prime's spark carried the powerful Autobot Matrix of Leadership, which granted him great powers of wisdom and strength, among other things, and the ability to destroy evil. (Watch 1986's *Transformers: The Movie* to see what I mean). Like the Holy Spirit does for the believer, Prime's spark granted Primal a new body and new powers. Like it was for Primal, the Spirit's weeding out of sin in the believer's life can be agonizing.

The transformed Primal led the Maximals to victory over the Predacons. The Spirit can do the same in your life.

And that's just prime.

Quest of the Day

1. Read 2 Corinthians 5.

2. How has your life changed since you came to Christ? Journal about three things that are different now about you because of the Spirit's work.

3. Identify an area the Holy Spirit is convicting you on as the next thing He wants you to change. Share this with a trusted friend and set up a time to meet and/or talk about this to keep you accountable.

DAY 39: PRAYER DAY 4

In the last few days you have been learning about God's calling for us to be new creatures and to share Him with others. Here are some prayer prompts.

Start with worship. Sing a song. Read a Psalm. Focus on how amazing God is and His grace and love.

Day 35 was a chance to learn how the Holy Spirit came to indwell believers. Ask Him to fill you with His freshness and love.

On Day 36 you read about Paul's conversion and were challenged to seek out a subculture you are part of to minister within. Pray for ministries you found that reach this subculture.

Next, pray for individuals you regularly meet with in this culture, even if you only see them every few months. Pray that they will experience Jesus or hear about Him.

On Day 37 you were challenged to do some acts of kindness for those different from you. Think of someone you know who is involved in other hobbies and groups. Pray for them. Pray for physical healing, emotional health and spiritual growth. Give God time to bring individuals to mind.

Take some time to ask God if you need to apologize to someone you don't understand. Someone who confuses you with their viewpoint on the world. Pray for them and ask God for wisdom in relating to them. Be quiet for a bit and let write down any thoughts about this.

Day 38 was about being a new creation. Take some minutes and praise God for how much He has already done in you. Thank him for work He has done in your attitude or your habits.

The Quest of the Day on Day 38 challenged you to identify what God is currently working on. Talk with God about this process. Ask Him to bring to light motivations behind hat needs to change.

DAY 40: FURTHER UP AND FURTHER IN
BY NATHAN MARCHAND

> Then I saw a new heaven and a new earth, for the first
> heaven and the first earth had passed away, and there was
> no longer a sea.
> Revelation 21:1

The Last Battle, the seventh and final book in C.S. Lewis' *Chronicles of Narnia*, is arguably the *Avengers: Infinity War* of the series. Narnia's darkest hour had come. A devious ape named Shift disguised the unsuspecting donkey, Puzzle, in a lion skin and passed him off as a false Aslan (the mighty lion who serves as a Christ-figure). Shift deceives many Narnians, convincing them to serve the Calormenes and cut down Talking Trees. The Narnian king Tirian and his centaur friend Jewel investigate, killing a pair of Calormenes abusing a Talking Horse. Ashamed, they throw themselves at the mercy of who they believe is Aslan, only to discover it is Puzzle. Shift, now allied with a talking cat named Ginger and the Calormene warlord Rishda Tarkaan, declare that Aslan and the Calormene god Tash are one and the same. Tirian questions this, and he is tied to a tree. Desperate, he calls to Aslan for help.

He receives a dreamlike vision of the "Seven Friends of Narnia"—most of the children from the previous books. They can see him, too, but they can't speak to one another. Tirian awakes and is rescued by Eustace Scrubb and Jill Pole.

For the next several chapters, the heroes and villains gather forces. Shift and Tarkaan unintentionally summon the actual Tash to Narnia, dubbing him "Tashlan." They decimate the Narnian army. The warlord's forces clash with Tirian's group near a stable, but the few remaining Narnians loyal to Aslan are killed or sacrificed to Tash.

It's here we get that *Avengers* moment—the remaining Friends of Narnia appear dressed as Kings and Queens. Tash is banished and his minions defeated. But Aslan summons Father Time, who blows a horn and begins the destruction of Narnia. The stars fall from the sky; dragons eat the vegetation; Aslan passes judgment on all animals who lived in Narnia; finally, Father Time crushes the sun like an orange.

The door is closed to the "old Narnia," and the children are ushered into Aslan's Country—the "New Narnia." In the end of the book's penultimate chapter, it reads,

> It was the Unicorn who summed up what everyone was feeling. He stamped his right fore-hoof on the ground and neighed and then cried:
>
> "I have come home at last! This is my real country! I belong here. This is the land I have been looking for all my life, though I never knew it till now. The reason why we loved the old Narnia is that it sometimes looked a little like this. Bree-hee-hee! Come further up, come further in!"

He repeats this infectious phrase as he frolics throughout the beautiful meadows of Aslan's Country.

As they go "further up and further in," they meet the heroic mouse, Reepicheep, who'd gone with Aslan in *The Voyage of the Dawn Treader*, and he greets them by saying, "Welcome, in the Lion's name. Come further up and further in." Lucy is then reunited with Tumnus, the Faun from *The Lion, the Witch, and the Wardrobe*. Looking at the Garden before them, they have a chat that leads me to believe Mr. Lewis would've been a Whovian:

> "I see," she said at last, thoughtfully. "I see now. This garden is like the Stable. It is far bigger inside than it was outside."
>
> "Of course, Daughter of Eve," said the Faun. "The further up and the further in you go, the bigger everything gets. The inside is larger than the outside."

This leads to the novel's wonderful coda:

> And as He spoke He no longer looked to them like a lion; but the things that began to happen after that were so great and beautiful that I cannot write them. And for us this is the end of all the stories, and we can most truly say that they all lived happily ever after. But for them it was only the beginning of the real story. All their life in this world and all their adventures in Narnia had only been the cover and the title page: now at last they were beginning Chapter One of the Great Story, which no one on earth has read: which goes

on for ever: in which every chapter is better than the one before.

What makes this powerful is it mirrors the final chapters of the Bible. To say that the Book of Revelation is rife with nightmare fuel would be an understatement. The Archangel Michael battles Lucifer the Red Dragon during a "war in heaven" (Revelation 12:7) in a scene straight out of a high fantasy novel. Multi-headed, Lovecraftian beasts emerge from the sea and the Earth (Revelation 13). The terrifying "great harlot of Babylon" sits upon a scarlet beast (Revelation 17 NKJV). Stars fall from the sky. Plagues are unleashed. Angels dispense the wrath of God. "Human sacrifice, dogs and cats living together—*mass hysteria!*"

This is the inevitable future of the universe. A great cosmic unraveling. Evil's last assault on creation.

But in Revelation 19, Jesus Christ rides in on a white horse (v. 11) and sets everything right. He defeats the Beast and his armies and casts them into the "fiery lake of burning sulfur" (v. 20). In the following chapter, Christ reigns for a thousand years, Satan is thrown in the burning lake, and the dead are judged.

After all of these harrowing narratives, we finally reach the glorious climax that awaits those who remained loyal to Christ in chapter 21:

Then I saw "a new heaven and a new earth," for the first heaven and the first earth had passed away, and there was no longer any sea. I saw the Holy City, the new Jerusalem, coming down out of heaven from God, prepared as a bride beautifully dressed for her husband. And I heard a loud voice from the throne saying, "Now the dwelling of God is with men, and he will live with them. They will be his people, and God himself will be with them and be their God. He will wipe every tear from their eyes. There will be no more death or mourning or crying or pain, for the old order of things has passed away" (v. 1-4).

The world—indeed, the universe—will be transformed at this moment. Contrary to what many theologians have said, the current universe isn't destroyed and replaced by another one; it will be restored to what it was in Genesis. The corruption brought upon it by sin will be wiped away. God will dwell with humanity as He did in Eden.

Jesus declares to the Apostle John, the author of Revelation, "I am making everything new!" (v. 5a). It's this verse that inspired the subtitle of the book you're holding. The Bible culminates with a divine terraforming. Earth will become the paradise that was once lost, and Jesus' followers will reign with Him for eternity.

In his book *All Things New*, author John Eldredge writes extensively on this great restoration and how it gives hope to the Christian. We need to remember that this day is coming. Everything we lost will be restored. That was the point of these often confusing and weird stories in Revelation: Jesus and His followers win in the end. It isn't something to fear; the "birth pains" (Matt. 24:8; Mark 13:8) that come before it are incomparable to the joy that will follow. But as Eldredge tells his readers, eternity won't be boring. Like Aslan's Country, it will a renewed universe full of adventure that gets more exciting as we go "further up and further in." He encouraged his readers to not make a "bucket list," but a list of things they would do in eternity.

What's on your list?

<u>Quest of the Day</u>

1. Read Revelation 21.

2. Start a book club or book study group at your church for *All Things New* by John Eldredge.

3. As per Eldredge's advice, make a list of all the things you want to do when you reach this new heaven and new Earth. Let your imagination run wild. Do you want to explore other planets and visit other galaxies? Meet family and friends who "died in the Lord"? Read every book ever written? It can all be done!

DAY 41: ENDLESS WONDER!
BY ERIC ANDERSON

For the Lord most High is awesome, the Great King over all
the Earth.
Psalm 47:2

Warehouse 13 was a fun-filled, wonderful show. Its five seasons gave fans exciting adventures chasing magical artifacts all around the world: Edgar Allen Poe's Pen, Abraham Lincoln's Tophat, a Brick from the Berlin Wall, a Chinese Orchid, and many other items. (Unfortunately, I don't think they came upon a Mogui). Operatives of the Warehouse are encouraged to look for this "endless wonder" that comes from working there as they search for these items. They even time travel and at one point bring in author H.G. Wells, albeit with a major twist that only the *Warehouse* writers could think of. The show had some steampunk technology mixed with a few ancient myths and modern historical connections. They even made a point of going to the lost Library of Alexandria, which, in the show's mythos, had been the second Warehouse. In one episode we get a look at a new artifact being created. This happens in moments of extreme emotion, and Agent Claudia comes out of the experience mystified and filled with awe. The Warehouse is full of dozens of crazy and wonderful magical items, all of which can be dangerous.

The agents all live together in community at a large
house with a host who seems to always show up at the right
time. Cookies are used as a morale booster.

In Revelation we have a picture of creatures standing
around God's throne. One with a face like a man, one like an
eagle, one like an ox, and one like a lion. They keep yelling
again and again:

"Holy, Holy, Holy

is the Lord God Almighty

Who was, and is, and is to come"

(Rev. 4:8).

These creatures do this continuously, and one theory is that
they are constantly seeing something new in God. Exploring
different parts of who He is. One moment He creates a new
color. Another He grants mercy to a sinner who calls upon the
Name of Jesus. Yet another he heals a broken leg, and then He
brings someone out of a coma. On and on He goes creating,
re-creating, healing, granting hope, mercy, and grace to those
in need.

As for the throne itself, there are layers and layers of
beauty around it. Seven lamps burning, flashes of lighting,
rumblings, thunder, a rainbow that shines like an emerald,
thrones with elders plus the creatures mentioned above. A
magnificent throne room for an infinite God.

The 24 elders sitting around the throne are crying out:

"You are worthy, our Lord and God,

To receive honor and glory and power,

For you created all things,

And by your will they were created

and have their being" (Rev. 4:11).

What words do we use to describe God? Omnipotent: He is all powerful. Omnipresent: He is everywhere at every time. Omniscient: He is all-knowing. We are told that He knows every hair on our heads (Luke 12:7), and that He knew us in our mother's womb (Psalm 139:13-14).

We serve a God who is bigger, cleverer, and more amazing than we could possibly imagine. He never sleeps and never needs to eat, (although Jesus did eat, and I'm sure the Father can when He wants to). Do you want more? There will *always* be more! Do you think we'll spend eternity with Him just sitting there? Think about it. He is the King of Kings, the Lord of Lords, the Rose of Sharon, the Lord God Almighty, the Messiah, Emmanuel (God with us). He can create games out of his pinky finger that would enrapture every human ever to exist, or create a new language for us out of nowhere. He can create a galaxy with a single word or rebuild DNA any way He wants. He can create new music that would far surpass Bach, Beethoven, and the Beatles even if they all collaborated. He is the Alpha and the Omega, the only one worthy of all praise and honor and glory. God, the three in one—Father, Spirit, Son—who is and was and ever shall be.

This is the God of Endless Wonder.

<u>Quest of the Day</u>

1. Read Revelation 4 and Colossians 1:15-20.

2. Spend time worshiping Jesus in musical form, doing art to worship Him, or writing to Him in worship.

Day 42: The Unchanging God
By Nathan Marchand

Jesus Christ is the same yesterday and today and forever.
Hebrews 13:8

November 12, 2018, was "a day unlike any other." A day that would live in infamy in the nerd/geek community. The day a patriarch of geekdom passed from this mortal coil.

The day Stan Lee died.

I was sitting in the Writing Center for the university library when my little sister texted me the news. What started as a typical Garfield-style Monday for me as a hardworking graduate student quickly turned dark. I replied with a GIF of Toby Maguire crying in one of his Spider-Man films. She sent a GIF of Baymax hugging Hiro in the movie *Big Hero 6* with the caption, "You will be all right. There, there."

If you're reading this book, Stan Lee's significance doesn't need to be explained to you. If nothing else, you know him as the old guy who cameos in (almost) every Marvel movie. The man revolutionized comics in the 1960s, arguably saving the art form with the creation of characters like the X-Men, the Avengers, and Spider-Man, among many others. He later served as the publisher and president of Marvel Comics. Even after he retired in the 1990s, he became the face of the company. He was the surrogate grandfather of every "True Believer" (what he called Marvel Comic readers).

I had the privilege of meeting him at C2E2 in 2017. I'd heard that the then 94-year-old Stan would be retiring from convention appearances, so I knew I'd never get another chance to have him come this close to me ever again, so me and several of my friends day-tripped to Chicago. I spent my entire day focused on Stan, and I don't regret it. I saw him at a huge panel in the morning with fellow comics legend Frank Miller. He autographed my copy of *The Essential Captain America, Vol. 1* (I was cosplaying Cap, I might add). A friend and I had a photo taken with him. He even shook our hands when he shouldn't have. That photo has hung in my study ever since.

When he died, people talked about the characters he created, the stances he took against prejudice, and his love for the fans, and rightfully so. For me, though, the greatest lessons I gleaned from Stan's life hardly anyone discussed. First, he was nearly 40 years old when he hit it big with the publication of *Fantastic Four* #1—the official birth of the Marvel Universe— in November 1961. He'd worked at Marvel for over 20 years, having taken the job because it was a job, but had never been able to tell the kinds of stories he wanted to tell. He was on the verge of quitting when he got this opportunity. It was his wonderful wife, Joan, who urged him to stay on. As a 30-

something writer who hasn't achieved the level of success he wishes he had by now, I take great comfort in knowing this.

Speaking of Joan Lee, she and Stan were married for almost *seventy years* before her tragic death in 2017. Seventy *years!* Many people nowadays can't even stay married for seventy *minutes*. It's heartwarming and encouraging to see a love that true and committed.

I once met a comic book writer at a convention who told his panel audience that the Stan Lee we saw in public—the loveable, hyperbolic, self-effacing showman espousing old-fashioned values—wasn't a persona. It was who Stan was.

When Eric and I set out to write this book, our goal was to show how God changes things, whether that be people, circumstances, or nations. For the last 41 days, you've been reading all about that. I wanted to close your journey by telling you that while God can change anything, He Himself doesn't change. Theologians call this the "immutability of God." We see this taught throughout Scripture:

"I the Lord do not change" (Malachi 3:6a).

Jesus Christ is the same yesterday and today and forever (Hebrews 13:8).

Every good and perfect gift is from above, coming down from the Father of the heavenly lights, who does not change like shifting shadows (James 1:17).

If we believe that God is holy and good, there is tremendous comfort in this. Unlike us, He doesn't change for the better or the worse. He doesn't change His mind on a whim. He isn't subject to time, for He exists outside of it. He doesn't need to change Himself based on new circumstances or information. If He ever appears to have changed His mind, such as in Exodus 32:14 or 1 Samuel 15:11-29, it's because He was responding to changing circumstances or to His people. It also means that the God we read about in Scripture is the same God we can pray to every day.

What I'm about to say I say knowing full well that Stan Lee was as fallible a human being as all of us. *Star Trek: The Next Generation* actor Wil Wheaton even said in his tribute to Stan on Twitter that "Stan Lee was a complicated man with a complicated life." But I do think that Stan's steadiness—his devotion to Joan and his fans and the Marvel brand, his consistency of character in public and behind closed doors— is a reflection of God's immutability. A few days after he died, I saw a video interview of him from the 1960s, and despite him having a full beard and no glasses, I knew it was him. Why? Because he was still the lovable storyteller I saw in his last Twitter video where he thanked his fans for all their devotion. Comic writer Gail Simone said it best:

> Under the persona, Stan Lee was a real human being. I met
> him three times and three times he told me something

literally life-changing. I hope everyone knows, he cared about us. That was no act.... We were lucky to have him. Untold millions of lives made better by stories. Endless people who learned responsibility from Spider-Man, acceptance from the X-Men, self-forgiveness from the Hulk. Stan Lee put better heroes in our vision.

If we can trust that Stan Lee, imperfect though he was, could remain steady throughout his life, how much more can we trust in a truly immutable God?

Excelsior!

Quest of the Day

1. Using either Google, the YouVersion app, or another research tool, do a topic search for the "immutability of God." Read through those verses.

2. Journal about a consistent through line God had with you at a particular time in your life. What was happening? What did God show you and/or tell you?

3. In response to everything you've read and experienced in the last 42 days, write down some areas of your life that are in need of newness. Share these with a friend.

APPENDIX: RECOMMENDED RESOURCES

All Things New by John Eldredge

Heaven, Earth, and the Restoration of Everything
You Love

The Red Sea Rules by Robert J. Morgan

10 God-Given Strategies for Difficult Times

Experiencing God by Henry and Richard Blackaby

Knowing and Doing the Will of God

Goliath Must Fall by Louie Giglio

Winning the Battle Against Your Giants

Faith & Fandom Series by Hector Miray

Finding God in Geek Culture

Holy Heroes by Scott Bayles

The Gospel According to DC & Marvel

No Cape Required by Kristen Parrish

52 Ways to Unleash Your Inner Hero

YouVersion Bible App

www.First15.org

ACKNOWLEDGEMENTS

It takes a fellowship to destroy a magic ring, and it took a fellowship to make this new devotional possible. Nick Haden, Jennifer Shlamuess-Perry, and Scott Bayles all gave valuable feedback on the rough draft, for which we thanks you all. Thanks to Ruth Pike-Miller for once again creating amazing cover art for us. This book wouldn't be possible without events like GenCon, GrandCon Gaming Convention, Fantasticon, Michigan Statewide Teen Convention, MuskeCon, Intersect Youth Lock-In, and many others that have been accepting of a gentle expression of faith and fandom and have allowed us to table there to sell our books. Many friends and family have encouraged us on this road: Darrin Ball, Darren Anderson, Joy Lyle, Jennifer and Cory Ellison, Paul Boxer, Thad Spring, Dallas and Celeste Mora, and Becky Smith are just a few of them. For those we forgot to mention, let us know so you can be in the next book!

ABOUT THE AUTHORS

Eric "Mister" Anderson is a substitute teacher by day and Nerd Chapel's founder by night. His top three fandoms are *Stargate*, *Star Wars*, and *Doctor Who*, but he also enjoys board games, kaiju movies, DC & Marvel, and traveling. He attended Taylor University Fort Wayne (where he met Nathan) and earned a B.A. in Biblical Studies and Christian Education. He currently resides in Fruitport, MI. In addition to his B.A., he is a graduate of a Youth with a Mission Discipleship Training School and has been on many missions trips. His other areas of ministry include leading Bible studies and tech ministry (sound/lighting for services). You can find more of his insights of nerd-dom and faith at www.nerdchapel.blogspot.com or at www.facebook.nerdchapel.com. Nerd Chapel is also on YouTube. Contact him through the FB page for info on speaking or tabling at your event.

"Super" Nathan Marchand hails from Fort Wayne, Indiana. Homeschooled from an early age, he has loved speculative fiction since age three and discovered his talent for writing in sixth grade English. He attended Taylor University Fort Wayne, earning a B.A. in professional writing. He's currently studying for his M.A. in English. He's worked as a reporter in a small town, a feature writer for www.Examiner.com and www.GigaGeekMagazine.com, and as a freelance writer, among other things. His first novel, *Pandora's Box*, was published in 2010 by EDGE Science Fiction and Fantasy. He's also the co-creator of both the ongoing fantasy serial *Children of the Wells* (www.ChildrenoftheWells.com) and the podcast Kaijuvision Radio (www.Kaijuvision.com). He also occasionally makes YouTube videos. When not writing, he enjoys other creative endeavors like ballroom dancing, photography, acting, and occasionally saving the world. His website is www.NathanJSMarchand.com.

Made in the USA
Monee, IL
03 October 2021